W9-BFE-893

HOROSCOPES

HONOR ONE

HOROSCOPES
YOUR
DAILY FATE
AND FORTUNE

ZODIAC
PRESS

Copyright © 1983, Ottenheimer Publishers, Inc.
All Rights Reserved. Printed in U.S.A.

Contents

Birthday

Love, Romance & Marriage

Family & Friendship

Contents of
Birthdays

Introduction

INTRODUCTION

If this book were a history of Astrology many pages could be filled with the story of famous seers from Chaldean civilization in the ancient land of Ur up to the present day who ruled the destiny of nations by the way of the stars.

From those venerable times to the present, great minds have noted the influence of each planet in its dominance over the lives of men, and no living being is too remote for this control.

This book offers a simple analytical guide based on modern accepted conclusions, all of which will answer everyday questions.

People search the stars to find out if they are going to make lots of money, enjoy good health, and indulge in a glamorous love affair. They want a specific answer to concrete questions, such as:

Are we going on a cruise?
Is Tara getting the mink coat?
Will Stacey win a scholarship?
Is it going to be profitable for Andrew to major in chemistry?
Will Dad get a bonus next year?
Is Aunt Susan's operation a necessity?
Will stocks go up?
Will Uncle John leave me his money?
Will Kimberly's boyfriend propose, and is his father really rich?

Material questions? Perhaps. But all of these and thousands more clamor for answer. Your horoscope will illuminate the path.

Consider your horoscope as a searchlight trained on life, and in its radiance, once we have learned the code, the past is explained, the present clarified, and the path of the future outlined.

It is false to believe that the astrological plan sets the final hand of fate upon events and people, or that such a thing as bad luck is ordained. This is not true. Your horoscope never says "It can't be done," or "You are completely out of luck." Rather, it tells us what can be done, how and when; and in the words of an old quotation, "The stars incline, but they do not compel."

By all this is meant that the stars in their courses and the planets in their signs and heavenly houses have each a different influence upon our earthly life. These rays or vibrations cause us to be hasty or slow, bright or dull, calm or explosive, according to their force. The planets bring conditions to us, conditions of wealth or poverty, atmospheres of joy or sorrow, conflict or expansion.

All of these astrological forces help to shape our thoughts, which in turn direct our actions. Rash explosive attitudes that suddenly overwhelm can always be justified by the person afflicted.

"The occasion demanded that outburst," the person involved will declare.

It is such conditions that can be averted. If we are warned that rash actions will be the result of certain planets in their relation to the life, no matter how deceptively right that behavior appears to us at the time, we can hold a check on our emotions, and save the situation.

There is no combination of circumstances or emotions that is not conveyed to us by the heavenly bodies. When we know what to expect from these forces, we can use the energy and take advantage of the opportunities offered us by the stars.

First of all, clear every image out of your mind's eye and look up at the heavens.

Try to see it as a huge map of another world, with continents, countries, and principal cities, for that is what it really is; another World, made up of twelve Heavenly Houses, twelve signs of the Zodiac, and the ten major Planets.

The Heavenly Houses, twelve in number, are like continents. They are stationary, and each house has an environment, or a special atmosphere all its own.

Traveling in and out among the Heavenly Houses are the twelve Signs of the Zodiac. Each sign has its own influence which combines in meaning with whatever House it happens to be in at the time of the transit.

Lastly, the ten Planets, weaving around the Zodiac, add their mighty influence to the Signs and Houses.

Therefore, every individual's character is a combination made up of House, Sign and Planet, according to the picture of the heavens on the day of his or her birth.

Some people are mirrors of their sun sign; others, where the moon is well aspected, take dominant characteristics from the moon. Still others are influenced by the ascendant.

The following chapters will describe the meaning of each House, Sign and Planet. After that, individual birthdays will be analyzed.

In order to get a complete horoscope, the following is necessary:

A Solar reading, which is based on the individual birthday.

A Lunar reading, which is based on the position of the moon—the year, month and day of birth.

A reading of the Ascendant, which is based on the hour of birth.

Zodiac

THE TWELVE HOUSES OF THE ZODIAC

These twelve heavenly houses are often called "Palaces of the Sky." At birth, each planet is in a sign, and both planet and sign are posited in a heavenly house. The law governing this is as follows:

The first house belongs to the first sign, which is Aries. The second house to Taurus. The third to Gemini, the fourth to Cancer. The fifth to Leo. The sixth Virgo. The seventh to Libra, the eighth to Scorpio. The ninth to Sagittarius, the tenth to Capricorn. The eleventh to Aquarius, and the twelfth, to Pisces.

These house and sign relationships are harmonious to each other, and lucky is the person who is born with the signs posited in their rightful houses.

Since people are born every day in the year, and the constant journey of signs and planets is unceasing as the train moves through the houses around the Zodiac, it is quite usual for births to occur in heavenly houses harboring, at that moment, an antagonistic sign to that particular house.

For this reason many lives carry a spirit of discord throughout the span. It is said that a lack of ability to accept and conform to the world we live in shows a poor quality of mind. Many of the people who cannot adjust themselves to their environment might be better able to do so had they an understanding of their natal horoscope.

The meaning of the twelve heavenly houses is as follows:

The first house is the house of personality.

The second house is the house of wealth.

The third house is devoted to relationships between brothers and sisters, neighbors and close relatives. Short journeys, messages, and communications are also third-house matters.

The fourth house deals with the home. This includes family life, the mother, and all the events connected with home life.

The fifth house holds the love life. It takes in pleasures, romantic experiences, entertainment, and includes all children in the life of the native.

The sixth house is the house of health, work and service. Grandparents and all other elderly relatives, pets, family dogs and cats, live stock, servants, and useful possessions are sixth-house possessions.

The seventh house is the house of marriage and partnership.

The eighth house holds death, rebirth and, logically enough, inheritance. It should be mentioned here at the very beginning that astrologically, death is a passing, or a disposition of, and may be the completion of a cycle, or the end of a condition, as well as the passing of a person.

The ninth house harbors the bigger things of life. Philosophy, and religion in the realm of mind and spirit, and big business, world travel, and high-pressure gambling in the flesh. It includes expansion in all fields.

The tenth house is the house of business, government, and

the hard hand of authority. It is also the Patriarch of the houses, symbolizing the Father.

The eleventh house belongs to friendship, social programs and reforms.

The twelfth house is the house of secrets, silence, enemies and isolation.

These heavenly houses influence life in the following way:

At birth the signs and planets are posited in various houses.

The atmosphere of the house blends with planet and sign to make an influence. In addition, the planets make what is known as aspects to each other. The house, as well as the sign and planet, is affected by these aspects.

Aspects are forces that give energy to the original meaning of the sign, house, planet combination. These aspects are benign or explosive, and are called trines, squares or oppositions. The trines are slow motion, but harmonious, while the squares are explosive, and create conflict. Sometimes the violent square results in greater fortune and richer results than the happy trine.

There are also conjunctions, where two planets are found in the same sector of the sign, or in conjunction. This aspect combines the meaning of both, the stronger planet infecting the more variable. There is also the harmonious semi-sextile, and the sextile.

If a heavenly house in an individual horoscope suffers from an explosive aspect at birth, the person feels activity in that particular department of the life throughout their span of years. For instance, if at birth the fourth house, holding Uranus makes an opposition to the native's sun, the home life of that person will always incline toward lightning changes. Uranus is the planet of upheaval and violent reorganization. The individual, learning this fact, must recognize that changes can be made for the best, but quick action is essential.

Every aspect has a positive and a negative reaction. It is the force behind the influence that is valuable. An explosive aspect has that very useful energy, which to some of the passive signs and planets is just the needed impetus to make progress.

Never be frightened by a square or opposition. Frequently right thinking, and correct action applied to these violent forces result in success.

The promising trine often lulls us into a dreamy, inactive mental attitude. Then the favorable period passes without result from the good opportunity presented, and is followed by a violently antagonistic period that could never be used for gain, but is energy that might after all, be useful in another field.

THE TWELVE SIGNS OF THE ZODIAC

The signs of the Zodiac are divided into fire, water, earth and air signs, and partake of the qualities of those elements.

The fire signs are Aries, Leo and Sagittarius.

The water signs are Pisces, Cancer, and Scorpio.

The earth signs are Taurus, Virgo, and Capricorn.

The air signs are Gemini, Libra and Aquarius.

Each of the twelve signs rules a different part of the human body, making this organ strong or sensitive according to the birth aspects and lunations current throughout the life.

The first sign of the Zodiac is Aries, the Ram, ruled by Mars, and is the sign of leadership. It is the sign of the fearless pioneer and creator, as well as renewed life and idealistic accomplishment. Aries governs the head and face.

The second sign of the Zodiac is Taurus, the Bull, the sign of wealth, real estate and property. Venus rules this sign, making it also the sign of love and beauty. Taurus rules the neck and throat.

The third sign of the Zodiac is Gemini, the Twins, sign of the dual personality, brother and sister, short journeys, speed, messages, communications. The mind, perceptions, and developed intellect are part of this sign. The Ruler is Mercury. Gemini governs the shoulders, arms and hands.

The fourth sign of the Zodiac is Cancer the Crab, sign of the home and mother. In a minor way this takes in small business deals, and dictates the disposition in home and business life. Cancer is ruled by the moon. Governs the stomach and breast.

The fifth sign of the Zodiac is Leo, the Lion, sign of Love, and quite properly children. This is the sign of pleasure, adventure, sports, speculation, showmanship and romance. It is the sign of good times, holidays, and good fellowship. Leo is ruled by the Sun, and governs the heart.

The sixth sign of the Zodiac is Virgo, the Virgin—sign of health, work, and service. Virgo is the sign of duty to the aged and infirm, honest servitude, and care of the health. Mercury is the ruler, and governs the intestines.

The seventh sign of the Zodiac is Libra, the Scales, the sign of partnership and marriage, diplomatic relationships, and foreign affairs. Libra is ruled by Venus, and governs the kidneys in men, and the ovaries in women.

The eighth sign of the Zodiac is Scorpio, the Scorpion, sign of death, and regeneration, wills, inheritances and conditions surrounding the natives' own passing. Scorpio is ruled by Pluto, and governs the organs of generation.

The ninth sign of the Zodiac is Sagittarius, the Archer, sign of great philosophies and religion. Expansion in all forms, extravagant enterprise, big business, and world-wide commerce comes under Sagittarius. The ruler is Jupiter, governing hips and thighs.

The tenth sign of the Zodiac is Capricorn, the Goat, sign of success, authority, paternal and governmental. Worldly position, fame, and recompense are measured by Capricorn. The sign ruler is Saturn, who governs the knees.

The eleventh sign of the Zodiac is Aquarius, the Water-Bearer, sign of friendship. Aquarius indicates the quality of the social code in man's connection with associates, the degree of humanity, and the civilization of the individual. Ruled by Uranus, who governs the legs.

The twelfth sign of the Zodiac is Pisces, the Fishes, sign of secrets and secret enemies, isolation, imprisonment and tears. Pisces determines the spiritual burdens and repressions, also the sacrifices of the native. Ruled by Neptune, governing the feet.

THE PLANETS

THE SUN—YOURSELF.
RULER OF LEO. POWERFUL IN ARIES.

The sun represents the most powerful influence in human life. Like the old popular song, "It's not your nationality, It's not your personality, It's YOU." The real you, hidden beneath the veil of your personality and appearance. In astrology, as in nature, the sun is the vital principle behind life and growth.

The sun indicates the ultimate goal or ambition in the life. Whether or not this ambition is achieved rests with the quality of the aspects made by other planets to the sun. A well aspected sun will give singleness of purpose, and strength and energy to the life, as well as the ability to carry the ambition to a successful fulfillment. With a poorly aspected or afflicted sun the native often misses the mark. In a woman's horoscope the sun's position reveals her success with men.

THE MOON—YOUR TEMPER AND YOUR TEMPERAMENT.
RULER OF CANCER. STRONG IN PISCES.

The moon is your disposition, your moods and your fan. cies. The moon governs your point of view and the way you adjust yourself to the life, and to all situations and contacts coming the way of mankind. If the moon in your birth horoscope suffers from bad aspects, you will find it a struggle to get along with people all of your life. When the sun and moon are not harmonious, the life is filled with conflict, and success often just passes by.

The moon controls scandal, sensational gossip, and all appeals to the masses. In a man's horoscope the moon's position outlines his measure of success with women.

The Moon shares importance with the Sun in a horoscope, and every person should seek out the position of the Moon in his chart. We will help everyone to find the position of his or her natal Moon in this book.

JUPITER—THE BIGGER THINGS OF LIFE.
RULER OF SAGITTARIUS—POWERFUL IN PISCES.

The Planet Jupiter, called by the ancients, "The Greater Fortune," represents religious urges, philosophical thoughts, and dreams of vast accomplishment and great ideals. Jupiter controls journeys on foreign seas, world travel, and money and power gained through great enterprise. Gambling in material coin as well as speculative thought is part of the Jupiter character. The personality of Jupiter is jovial, expansive, generous and benign. The sign and house in which it is found in the horoscope tells where and how much of the world's material goods will be forthcoming during the lifetime. Jupiter also, wherever posited, characterizes the quality of thought of the individual.

VENUS—LOVE, BEAUTY, AND THE SOCIAL WHIRL.
RULER OF TAURUS AND LIBRA. FRUITFUL IN PISCES.

Venus, having in a more material sense many of the qualities of Jupiter, has been called "The Lesser Fortune." Venus, too, governs according to the position in the horoscope worldly goods, in the form of money, jewels, and all the luxuries of life. Venus colors the personal appearance, the personality, and the degree of success in the social world. Venus controls the love life; not entirely, it is true, as other planets have a part in this glamorous adventure. But the position and quality of the Venus does decide at least one-half of the native's experiences in the charming world of love and romance. It dictates your ability to attract and hold admirers, your general popularity, and lastly your capacity for spending money.

With an afflicted Venus a person might find himself self-indulgent to the point of vice, or quarrelsome with sweethearts, dogged by scandal, and deluged with bills caused by his own incurable extravagance.

MARS—THE BATTLEFIELD.
RULER OF ARIES AND SCORPIO.

Mars means a hard fight against everything that you hate. This force gives courage and the strength to go in and conquer enemies. The thorny paths and the conflicts are always stimulating to Mars, who thrives on debate, controversy and battle.

Mars is the planet of hard work and accomplishment, and always expresses activity, restlessness and the will to tackle a problem. Mars is such a violent physical force that it must be harnessed to progressive, useful activity in the life; otherwise the result is apt to be destructive. The personality of the planet is motion, explosion and war. Naturally, energy of this type must have a moral motivation. When good is the goal, the results are wonderful, but undirected; some of the most shocking murders, and bloody battles have been the result of the Mars force.

NEPTUNE—THE PLANET OF DELUSION, DREAMS AND VISIONS.
RULER OF PISCES—STRONG IN CANCER.

Neptune represents the dreams, visions and secret castles in Spain. Again, the sign and house indicate what this castle is built of, how it is furnished, and when it will materialize. Neptune rules the dreams of impossible sugar-loaf cottages, as well as fine marble palaces, and lastly the soul chambers for the spiritual house.

The Neptune influence is delicate and subtle. A little of the poetic, mystical Neptune quality makes the average person interesting. Life with its hard realism needs Neptune's unearthly charm to soften and humanize, but when the Neptune quality is too dominant in the life it brings evils that the world censures harshly.

When the Neptune character deals with soft humanizing pity, it aids reforms, but when "the soft influence" goes too far, we have drug addicts, perverts, drunkards and persons whose capacity for deception is so boundless and hard to fathom that it can only be called "the psychopathic case."

The scope of Neptune is wide for both good and evil, dealing as it does with those inmost reaches of the soul with which the average man has little patience and less understanding. Neptune badly aspected saps the energy, and devitalizes the mind. Neptune exalted makes a divine fire so delicate as to be beyond the comprehension of the rank and file of humanity.

MERCURY—RULER OF THE INTELLECT.
RULER OF GEMINI AND VIRGO.

This planet is an intellectual force controlling the mentality. It also rules common sense, and is a symbol of what you think and how you express your thoughts. The quality of the mentality is, of course, subject to the sign and house where Mercury is found in each horoscope, and its possible conjunction with other planets.

Mercury controls quick thinking, glib accurate expression of thoughts, colorful language, and an accurate grasp of any situation. Mercury has brilliancy, understanding, and powers of faultless execution of any task or problem set for solution. The intellect is cold, abstract, but honest, and the execution of manual work, perfect. Mercury governs speed, communications by word or wire, journeys short and fleet, in fact, as the Ancients described him, he is "the messenger of the gods."

Badly aspected, this fine dispassionate intellectual force and smart coordination of body and mind can be turned into forces that lie, steal, dupe and forge with a slickness that, like the magician's wand, eludes detection in its polished adroitness.

URANUS—THE PLANET OF FREEDOM.
RULER OF AQUARIUS.

"Let Freedom Ring" is the banner of Uranus. All the urges directing a person toward upheaval, complete change, and the upward climb to the light of freedom are controlled by Uranus. By this is meant that Uranus coldly destroys restraint and breaks down the barriers of convention, particularly outworn restrictions and passé conventions.

The planet Uranus rules what might be called "The Greater Mind," Mercury being in control of the "Lesser Mind." The Uranus vibration suggests connection with advanced planes of thought, gathered from a loftier existence in a planetary system as yet unstudied. Uranus is the most occult of the planets, and injects into the life of this world new codes, new laws, and new social orders. However revolutionary the new standards of Uranus may seem, they are in complete harmony with the divine plan. Badly aspected, a Uranus upheaval is malignant and devastating.

PLUTO—PLANET OF DEATH.
RULER OF SCORPIO.

Pluto is the planet of death, regeneration, and reform. Pluto governs sex and reproduction—also wills, legacies, and inheritances. The personality of Pluto is dark, cold, and sorrowful. The Pluto type of death is usually from natural causes, illness, decay or old-age. Life under Pluto passes silently from this plane into the unknown. It might be recalled that in Greek mythology Pluto was the king of the underworld, dark and turgid, but at a special plea of mankind he allowed his wife Proserpina to visit the earth every year. Her coming was a rebirth of joy, and we call it springtime. As has been explained, Pluto removes conditions as well as persons, and starts the tide of rebirth.

In matters of reform Pluto is unlike Uranus. The Pluto type of reformation takes the form of penance.

On the worldly plane, Pluto governs the execution of wills, legacies, and inheritances.

SATURN—THE OLD MAN OF THE ZODIAC.
RULER OF CAPRICORN.

The planet Saturn has been called "The Great Malific," The Disciplinarian of the Zodiac, and The Old Man of the Zodiac. In Saturn is vested all the ills the flesh is heir unto, delays, obstacles, disappointments, illness, trouble, and frustration. Saturn halts progress, limits returns, saps energy, weakens health, and curtails freedom.

To wrest any favor from Saturn mortal mind must be pure and uncontaminated. Human behavior must be dutiful and sacrificial. Then Saturn rewards with power and authority. Sometimes the reward is fame and high worldly position.

The Saturn personality is wholly frigid, repressed and unsympathetic. The vibrations differ from the abstract mental principle of Uranus, or the Spiritual illusions of Neptune.

The Saturn influence is a stern tonic for the soul, out of which only the strong can wrest rewards.

Birthday

Aries

March 21—April 19th

Inspiration leads you
to seek new worlds
to conquer.
Your happiness lies
in a victory over limiting conditions.
The conquest
is your source of greatest happiness,
and you cheer
when you win.
Once that's accomplished
you're bored
and seek some new way to find challenge
and get the best of it.
You rejoice at overcoming hindrances,
defeating obstacles and opposition.
This goes for love, too;
watch out a bit
for this happiness trend,
preferably by marrying someone
who gives you a constant sense of challenge.
You can be joyous
when striving
to win political position
and each step upward
in this field
can provide splendid challenge.

YOUR BIRTHDAY IN ARIES

Aries is the first sign of the Zodiac, and represents the springtime of life. Mars is the ruler, and he starts the battle as a shining young soldier on fire with the principle of the Holy Grail.

Aries people are natural leaders, with the courage, energy, and originality necessary to inspire followers. They are often topheavy with personality, and are well able to carry out all of their plans. That they begin ventures and leave the finishing to others is also part of the Aries character. They start great things, and are the "Doers" of the world, but other great ideas inspire them before their work is completed. This quality is acceptable when they have become the exalted of the earth, where there are plenty of minions to do the detail work.

However, the sign produces two types of persons, both as to appearance and character; the pure type, which is noble, and the mixed, which is weak, futile, sheeplike, and in all things a faint copy of his classic brother.

27

Physically, the pure Aries type is a proud looking person, with a fine carriage, and a clean high-bred profile. They have beautifully shaped facial bones and a bold prominent nose. Their coloring is fair or tawny, with cool blue eyes. A great many red-heads are found among Aries people. They have muscular bodies, and move with agile grace, suggestive of tremendous energy and virility.

The pure Aries type of man, having all of the above characteristics, is handsome but unapproachable—"Hard to get" is the popular term. The Aries woman has a frosty, aristocratic style of beauty.

The mixed Aries type follows this description much diluted. A blend is produced by a weak Sun, or a powerful Moon and a strong ascendant. Any number of combinations can modify a type.

A little softening of the dominant Aries nature can be a good thing, for the Aries person is hard to live with. They are so violent, demanding and aggressive that despite all of the excitement with which life with Aries natives is filled, the strain of keeping pace with them is too great. Therefore it is easy to see how a gracious Libra Moon, or even a gentle Cancer influence, or a noble Sagittarian ascendant might mellow the temper of the Aries character.

But if you are an Aries person, you may expect to find yourself basically as described here—fearless, ardent, energetic, vital, inventive, intellectual and idealistic on the good side of the ledger. On the bad side, there will be impatience, rashness, temper, violence, and emotional storms.

It is quite true that great leaders have come from the Aries group, in all fields of endeavor, so that an Aries person with the will to stick to a task until it is completed has many opportunities in life.

Although the Aries fertile mind lives all through the life, the Aries person seldom accumulates money until middle age. They may make plenty of money when quite young, but it seldom has a chance to pile up until late in life. They are extravagant people, not so much because they coddle and baby themselves—they never do that—but because beautiful surroundings, smart clothes, and a generally luxurious front make them feel powerful and confident, and more able to succeed in their work. No spur of necessity for them.

More than one marriage is often necessary to find happiness for the Aries man and woman. They are not easy to live with, and when very young make unsuitable selections of sweetheart or mate. If events make it possible for them to make a choice of a mate when they are about thirty-five years old, the chances of choosing wisely are good. It must be remembered that they bring a vital spark into marriage that makes them interesting partners. "Never a dull moment" has been used to describe the Aries partner.

More Aries people suffer from accidents than natives of any other sign of the Zodiac. Especially accidents to the head and face. They must always be more careful when driving planes, motor cars, power boats, or any speedy craft, than any other person undertaking the same task. This is also true of the Aries person in sports, especially games where there is an element of danger. For the native of any other sign it is a sporting chance; for Aries, it is a risk. They shine, but they take a chance.

Aries people are poor gamblers. By this we mean that they are unfitted by temperament and planetary conditions for any game of chance where money can be won or lost They seldom win, and almost always lose. If the game were such that it could be won by plans—schemes and logical thought—the Aries native could win, but where the Angels of Chance preside, Aries is OUT. Definitely, he is not their "Baby."

Although qualities of early youth remain with Aries people until old age, they are not among the very old people of the Zodiac. Frequently they wear themselves out before their time. They should heed warnings against over-eating as age advances. They should go in for plain food, moderately sized meals and quieter lives, else apoplexy will result. They can lengthen their lives if they will tone things down as the years pile up.

Taurus

April 20th —May 20th

You are quite steadfast
in your view
of happiness.
To win and hold an ideal,
cherished lifemate,
to rear a family
of which you can be proud,
to hold valuable property
and have a solid savings account
are all in the nature of happiness for you.
You like the applause of friends and associates
for work well done
and for careful thought
which allows you
to give good advice.
It pleases you
to be consulted frequently.
You are happy
when you feel
your life is secure
with the benefits you have won.
You have no objection
to some fame and honor of wider type
and may strive for it.
You are a worker
and just rewards give you happy gratification.

YOUR BIRTHDAY IN TAURUS

If you were born in this sign, ruled by lovely Venus, you are bland, expansive, loving and contented, a fine contrast and balance wheel for the high strung types of the Zodiac.

The Taureans make devoted husbands and loving wives, even though Taurean men and some of the women have been described as immoral. Love is very real to them, and they find the appeal of physical charm over-powering. None the less they take legal responsibilities seriously, and however the fancy may wander, they remain true to social and financial obligations throughout the life.

The Taurean home is a happy place to live in, luxurious, comfortable and restful. Often, it is in the country, with beautiful scenery surrounding it. Home or business, with the Taurean, is always run with practical efficiency.

The grace of Venus enriches Taurus characters to such an extent that they have the gift of making people welcome, so that many seek them out for the warmth of their companionship and the sincerity of their sympathy. One can always get advice from a Taurus person, and when it can be given, concrete financial help. He or she is generous, practical, worldly, and good.

This type of Venus influence is exceedingly material and places a high value on money, property, position and popularity. Taureans like to fill their homes with hosts of people, for they are hospitable, but they will not fail to flatter the wealthy and beautiful far beyond the poor and obscure. They are lion hunters, and like to be associated with the affluent and popular of the world.

The primitive Taurus character is not such a happy product. Badly aspected, the low Taurus type is ruthless and destructive, brutish, and blind to reasoning. The primitive Taurus woman is mercenary, slovenly, over-indulgent and immoral—A Frowsy Venus. The lowest of these types are infrequent, and it is the handsome, dependable, well-groomed Taurus native that we meet in daily life.

Taurus people gravitate to the country, and find their occupation in farm life whenever possible. They make excellent farmers on a huge scale, developing fruit farms, ranches, live-stock and poultry farms. They are great experimenters with cattle and fruit, in fact any growing thing, and are successful with modern dairies and produce of all kinds.

It seems as though the Taurus person, desiring so much wealth and comfort, has been fitted by nature with the patience and endurance to pursue success until he gets it. These people are often lucky. They win out in big expensive gambling games, and frequently win valuable prizes. They are temperamentally fitted for gambling, as they have steady nerves, great patience, and the much talked of "poker face."

In fact it is not only in gambling that some of these qualities are revealed. Taureans are the most patient people of all the Zodiac types, and will work and wait interminably for anything that they happen to want, especially if it is money or love. Their determination is colossal, and their ability to absorb insult just as great. If they are thrown out of one door they are sure to try the other. It is the force that wins.

The lower type of Taurus person makes an admirable servant. They are not debased by servitude, and their humbleness has a natural warmth that is not servile. They enjoy serving, and are faithful to the end.

The highest type of Taurean is not at all intellectual, but even when measured by the exacting standards of to-day their sense of beauty is of the highest type. High art decrees that no object can be truly beautiful that is not useful as well. All of the Taurean possessions including the home are built on this plan. It must be that the earth, which is exalted in the sign of Taurus, combined with the rulership of Venus brings about instinctive knowledge of what is beautiful.

In appearance the Taurus person is apt to be solidly built, but rather stocky. The men have tremendous strength, virility and endurance. Their bodies are the big-shouldered type with bulging muscles. The features are fleshy, and the complexion clear and exquisite. The whole face flushes readily, and the eyes, large and clear, sparkle with health. This applies to both sexes.

The health of Taureans is robust. Their natural relation to the earth seems to give them this almost superhuman strength and endurance. When illness does overtake them, they are ashamed to admit their weakness. To Taureans illness is a weakness, and they often endure a complaint until they can no longer throw it off. Then recovery is very slow, for the recuperative powers are not sufficient for resistance. The Taureans' throat is their most sensitive organ. They suffer from illnesses of the throat and contract any complaint affecting that organ.

The Taurus people of both sexes are naturally suited for matrimony and domestic life. Although as it has been pointed out, the senses may stray, the sense of obligation in a material way never deserts them. Besides, they are affectionate people, warm and loving, and the inconsistency of variety does not upset them.

The Taurus woman has a very loving and beautiful character. She blossoms with kind treatment and adores luxury. Her best qualities of contentment, affection, consideration, and gracious loving service come out when she marries a well-to-do man. It is not so much that she is mercenary, although the low, primitive Taurean is that too, but she is usually beautiful, or has the qualities of beauty, and she has learned to value herself. This is not vanity, but an old-fashioned feeling that she must be sheltered, catered to, and protected. In return, the Taurus wife and mother blends into the domestic background even better than the Cancer wife, who has her moody, exacting, over-sensitive, teary moments.

Among the Taurus charms is sometimes found a lovely singing voice. The throat, governed by this sign, frequently gives the world wonderful singers.

Gemini

May 21-June 21st

Your dual nature,
symbolized by the Twins in the zodiac,
finds happiness
in using swift wit
to solve problems ingeniously.
Your skills also being happiness
in artful endeavors,
You enjoy using eloquence to charm,
perhaps to win fame in your career,
A busy life keeps you happy
and the more variety
the greater is your elation.
Idleness or loneliness
depresses you.
You are happy on a journey,
entering a new group,
trying some new use
for your talents.
A new romance
exhilarates and pleases.
Be wary of
too much change,
scattered use of talents,
for these can lead to futility,
lack of joy.

YOUR BIRTHDAY IN GEMINI

The sign of Gemini, light as the air that gives it character, is the sign of the dual personality.

The average Gemini person is not the extreme case of split personality, where the subject dramatically changes from good Dr. Jekyll, to evil Mr. Hyde. But the Gemini native has, more than any other kind of person, two distinct natures. They blow hot and cold, are "with you, and agin' you," or they are sunshine and showers. All of these variable dispositions are found in Gemini more than in any other Zodiacal type.

At best, they are many-faceted people, sparkling, brilliant, and hard, like diamonds. They have the mental qualities inspired by the sign ruler, Mercury, fleet-footed messenger of the gods. This influence makes them intellectual, analytical, full of wit and accomplishments. The Gemini mind is impersonal, and never guided in decisions by emotions, or even qualities of right or wrong. But they do have a very wide stripe of common sense in their make up. They can think problems out for other people, for their approach is always rational, though cold.

Again, the influence of Mercury makes them very capable people. They can turn a hand to anything, and do it well. They always have a professional touch, and are nimble-fingered, skillful and adroit. They move quickly and gracefully, and are impatient with anything but high speed.

If a Gemini native is not employed in mental work, or some intellectual pursuit, but is found working at a skilled trade, more than likely it will be where great delicacy and dexterity are essential.

More often Gemini people are found in the legal profession, or writing for the newspapers. They make fine surgeons, dentists, or engineers, electrical and mechanical. They are adapted to radio mechanics, or airplane manufacture, for this sign is air-minded. They are also very mathematical, and make excellent certified public accountants. Many financial manipulators come from the sign of Gemini, and though to them the risks seem certainties, several fraudulent schemers have built up miraculous fortunes, only to have the law overtake them, to show up the airy miscalculations of their plans. A certain Mr. Ponzi, of doubtful fame was a native of Gemini who tangled himself up in one of these ventures.

The natives of this sign are socially in demand. Their temperament makes them appear gay and charming, even when within themselves they are not at all interested. They always appear sociable, and really do add to the success of any group, for they are witty and poised and highly stimulated by society.

They are usually very well informed, and apparently have plenty of information on any subject mentioned. This is not always true, but Gemini thinks so quickly and speaks so fluently that a very superficial knowledge goes a long way.

It is in a sense remarkable that these natives enjoy social popularity, for they are sharp-tongued and gossiping. Gemini people spread rumors, and they could fill a scandal sheet with tid-bits of gossip. Some serious backfires, and lively revenge has been the result of this loose chatter.

Gemini people are often good looking in a clear-featured, smart way. They have small neat features, nicely patterned in a long head. Their mien is animated and wide-awake, expressive of great intelligence. They are usually slender, and often very thin. They are exceedingly nervous, impatient and variable in manner and mood. This impatience is not the kind met with in the Aries native, who is restless because he cannot get his work done fast enough, but the Gemini impatience is rather the impatience of a bored person who, having started one thing, is now weary and desirous of starting something else.

The health of Gemini natives is usually excellent. They appear to be rather fragile, or at least delicate, but this is not the case. Doubtless that impression is created by the fact that they are so nervous and thin, and apparently wear themselves down to the bone. They seldom contract illnesses, and maintain a remarkably even grade of health. All this is true under average circumstances. With excessive strain, the lungs might be affected, as these are sensitive in Gemini.

The negative Gemini type has all of the detachment and coolness of his higher intellectual brother, but it falls to the degree of calculated cunning. This type often provides stock swindlers, confidence men, counterfeiters, forgers, and alas, blackmailers. The Gemini woman of the lower orders is the perfect gold digger. Her type appears to be the fragile pure madonna, who needs a strong arm to lean on because the hard world offends her matchless purity. Actually, this type is just cold rather than pure, but one effect can sometimes mask another.

In love and marriage Gemini men have the contrast of mild affections and sensual passions. The two qualities, within this sign, have little in common. As a lover, the native is arch, flirtatious, teasing and boyish. He is seldom vitally interested, and even when he is attracted, another personality can quickly charm him.

He is somewhat more satisfactory as a husband. Home ties do mean something to him, especially if he marries an intellectual companion. If however his wife is of the nagging, demanding, possessive type, the Gemini husband will not be able to endure it. He is temperamentally unfit to endure constant pressure. When Gemini men have overbearing wives, they often leave home. When they do not take such strong measures, they become that sad object, a hen-pecked husband.

Gemini women are exceedingly refined. They have a rare, unapproachable delicacy that is very attractive to wealthy men, who wish to have wives who suggest class and appear to be well bred. The disposition is sunny, the mind, active and agile, and the manner in society poised and charming. In private domestic life it is often a surprise to find so much animal passion in these fragile, bird-like women.

Cancer

June 22nd—July 23rd

When you are happy
in home and family conditions,
you really ask little beyond that
in the way of pleasure.
Good friends
and frequent entertainment
in your home
add to happiness.
You find joy
when preparing delicious meals in the kitchen,
in children whom you can instruct
and bring up in fine tradition.
When your children
do things
to make you proud,
you are in your glory
with radiant happiness.
Taking part in community events
fills you with happiness.
and being able to help others
with sympathetic understanding
also rates your happiness list.
Travel pleases when the family is along.
You are happy
in work with home essentials in your career,
working with food,
furnishings,
running a motel.

YOUR BIRTHDAY IN CANCER

The sign of Cancer is ruled by the Moon, and is exceedingly sympathetic to Neptune influences as well. In consequence, the Cancer types (and there are two distinct types) are the most moody, sensitive, impressionable of all the people of the Zodiac. They are whimsical, brooding, fanciful personalities, strongly instinctive, but very timid, and unwilling to face realities.

This is especially true of the feminine Cancer type. Perhaps at this point it might be advisable to classify the two varieties of this sign. One type might be called the masculine, the other the feminine. The masculine, or active type, differs in positive or active ways from the feminine or passive type.

The feminine type finds the harsh struggle for existence too much for its soft make-up. These people cannot find the strength to pit themselves against the world, and they seek the security of something stable upon which to pin their faith as well as their place in the world.

The home with its background of protective mother love

is a sacred shrine for the Cancer person of both types. The feminine type feels safety and a haven from the harsh world of reality. The masculine type reveres the meaning of home in all of the traditional suggestions of the word.

Both types have a great reverence for the past, and an exaggerated idea of its virtues. They see only glamorous living conditions in the Golden Age; that is, they recognize only the golden part. To them, the past means the "good old days," no matter how clear it is to the world of today that they were also "the bad old days."

The symbol of Cancer, the Crab, with its hard, protective shell, clinging tenacious claws and spasmodic movements, is a key to the Cancer character. They want to be shielded, protected, and given their own way, petted by the world, so that no breath of opposition adds to the problems of life.

Cancer people are responsive, full of sympathy for suffering or misfortune, and they respond with ready generosity to charitable appeals. This same instinct makes it possible for impostors to take advantage of them, as they would rather err on the side of giving too much than to refuse help because of doubt or skepticism.

Cancer people of the masculine type make good relief workers, and the charity that has a Cancer native at the head is usually well financed, with a large bank account. A Cancer director of this sort organizes appeals to the public, and always manages to make successful demands on the public pocket. The hospital or day nursery run by the Cancer influence is always in funds.

These people are good soap-box orators. Any cause strong enough to capture their interest will give them a crusading spirit. Considering the natural timidity of the sign-character, this is an admirable attitude, as it costs the Native a great deal to be so whole-souled and courageous when he is really frightened to death.

Cancer types are good business people. Despite the fact that the business world of today is an uncertain, adventurous world, full of new conditions and the very opposing pitfalls that Cancer fears above all things, they are more often wealthy and successful than the opposite. They are so insinuating and devious, and work in such a quiet undercover way, that their purpose is accomplished before the very forces of opposition that they fear so much are aware of what is happening. This is not dishonest, as it sounds, (although such methods can be used for crooked ends), but it is the natural way for Cancer persons to evade the things they cannot fight. Their temperament, shaped by the Moon and Neptune, does not permit them to use the positive force of Aries or Leo.

World commerce, especially lines of exchange, or trading, wholesale businesses of all kinds, and the manipulation of unions, or group workers are the best fields for the Cancer capabilities.

The arts always get a percentage of Cancer natives. It can be readily understood that the Moon's influence plus the spiritual Neptune urge would produce the temperament of artists in many fields. Whether the Cancer talents develop is largely a matter of the strength in the individual horoscope. This quality of persistently chipping away bits of a hard task, naturally part of Cancer's makeup, do aid in the final success. All of Cancer's creative work, whether in the realm of poetry, prose, music or painting, has emotional appeal, spiritual value, and fanciful artistic style.

After suggestions of this sort it is somewhat of a disappointment to learn that the typical Cancer personal appearance is not artistic, or even pleasing. The masculine type is large, poorly proportioned, without symmetry or grace. Clothes hang on Cancer bodies in an untidy way, giving a half-dressed appearance. They move with the uncertain, hesitant gait of the crab. The eyes are pale and full, and never look like the eyes of a healthy person. The hair, light or dark, is sheenless and sparse. The female type is shorter, but just as badly built. Modifications of the type that greatly improve this picture are happily, frequent. The moon is an impressionable planet, and often modified by any stronger influence well placed in the natal chart.

The Cancer influence is not one of health or vigor. The sign is not necessarily short-lived, but all through the life the vitality is low, and there is little resistance to disease. The stomach is weak and the appetite large, so that possible illness is increased by poor health habits.

This sign is decidedly religious. To the masculine type the mystery of life is a deeply spiritual urge, and they are constantly delving into problems of the soul and the depths of the unknown. The feminine type has not the initiative to think beyond the small limits of everyday life. She is concerned with those closest to her.

The domestic hearth is very important to the Cancer native. Marriage, a part of this department, is treated seriously by Cancer men and women. Well aspected, they revere home life and enjoy their family. Unlike the Taurus home, it is not always beautiful or even well equipped, but it has an old-fashioned charm very dear to the Cancer people themselves. The Cancer husband may be fussy and exacting, but he is also warm and affectionate. The Cancer wife may be moody, changeable, tearful, possessive, and passionate in her demands on the time and efforts of her family, but she is also sincerely devoted, and her intensity is very genuine.

The weakest type of Cancer woman is so unable to cope with life, so spineless, and totally unable to make a positive effort in any direction, that she all too frequently stops trying. In this sign are found a great many "Ladies of the Evening."

Leo

July 23rd—August 23rd

A high, leadership position,
the center of the stage,
the applause of the crowd
are matters of happy delight for you.
You love to manage things,
to be an authority.
Warm generosity
allows you to help many
and this gratifies your need for happiness.
You like your opinion
to be the basis for action by others,
your word to be law
in family matters.
A responsible position
in community or church concerns
make you happy
and you do your best
to win honors thus.
You're at the peak of happiness
when you know
you have a band of admiring,
loyal friends.
Using talents
to entertain and win praise
is another source of happiness
for you to tap.

YOUR BIRTHDAY IN LEO

The sign of Leo presents us with the most spectacular personality in the Zodiac. A superlative statement usually invites contradiction, but in this case a comparison of the different types will prove this characterization to be correct.

The Aries person, nearest to the Leo makeup, does not have the majesty, the regality, and ability to command respect combined with love, so much a part of the Leo personality. If Aries natives are princes of the Zodiac, Leo natives are the kings.

The sign of Leo, ruled by the Sun, reflects the character plainly shown in the symbol of the sign, Leo, the Lion. They are kingly people, heroic, and generous.

In appearance, they have a noble carriage. They are poised, commanding and gracious. The shape of the head is good, being neither too large nor too small. The features are usually high-bred, the eyes fine, and the hair tawny, golden or red. The figure is exceedingly elegant, and the limbs and extremities very finely modeled.

In this sign, as in Aries, the deviation from the high type is just a step down. Sometimes it is several steps down, but in any case, the primitive Leo type is a sort of caricature of his noble brother. This type has not the fine modeling of the noble type, but has rather a fleshy bulging figure, heavy and pompous in effect.

The high type of Leo personality is strongly executive. They have a natural command of any situation and can give orders, speaking frankly, and criticizing freely, often offending by bluntness rather than ill will.

There is no ill will in the Leo nature, and nothing small or petty either. Natives simply never see any reason to withhold an opinion, whether flattering or harsh. Despite the fact that because of this quality they are super-critical, their employees or domestics adore them, and work willingly, with a real effort to please and serve.

To Leo, the best the world offers is naturally his, not only for self-aggrandizement, although that does enter into it, but because the Leo instinct seeks the highest honors, the best job, the first place, and "tops" in everything.

Too often this is a just choice. The Leo intellectual equipment is sound. They have a natural comprehension of human problems, are generous and understanding, and have a lot of "heart."

From early youth upward they are not plodding students or even searchers after intellectual or abstract truth. That is the work of Libra, or Sagittarius, or even Aquarius. But Leo is the sign from which the instinctively emotional humanitarian springs. He loves people and life, and his leadership springs from the force of his will power to communicate this to the world. The world trusts and respects Leo.

These people are not the eternally precocious child type. That is found in Gemini or even Aries. This sign seeks early maturity, and plunges into the problems of life with zest and enthusiasm.

In the business world, Leo persons fill high executive positions. They often rise to the presidency of a bank, or great industrial enterprises. In politics especially, Leo types shine. In this department they can fulfill their zest for leadership. The theatre or any theatrical enterprise is, however, the very best choice for Leo. The sign rules amusement centers, and Leo qualities seek a field that gives them close contact with an audience. They make the ideal impresario. Many famous matinée idols were born in Leo, or had Leo in some important spot in the natal chart.

The advertising business too has certain branches, namely contact and sales, where impressive Leo types are successful. Whatever the Leo profession in the life, it had best be dominant, original and somewhat sensational.

On the negative side, the Leo personality, when primitive, is that of a swaggering bully. He blusters noisily in the business and home life. The truest description of this type is the Lion in "The Wizard of Oz," who upon the mildest counter-attack, broke down and sang, "If I only had the nerve." Alas, this is all too true, for the low Leo type is a braggart, a show-off and a faker.

Leo is the sign of love. Other signs have a love rulership, but it is a different kind of love. The Taurus love, Venus ruled, has an affectionate, fruitful, womanly quality, material, but warm and enveloping, an atmosphere, rather than a quality. The Libra love, Venus ruled, is the esthetic, discriminating love of mind. But Leo, ruled by the sun controls the love nature, and has the fiery, passionate love of the ideal lover, a man's love, compelling, masterful, and absorbing. It is not fruitful in itself, but it inspires and promotes fruitfulness in others.

Leo is the sign of pleasures, sports and entertainments, gala occasions, fêtes, picnics, etc. Every kind of enjoyment is ruled by Leo, and since everything connected with Leo is large, fulsome and generous, Leo people are apt to over-indulge. They often eat too much, and sometimes drink too much. The uncontrolled Leo types are warned against the use of drugs.

The Leo physique is sturdy and robust. It needs to be to stand the drains of the Leo temperament. They overwork. They undertake, somewhat like Aries people, tasks beyond human strength. They frequently dissipate in one way or another. They seldom heed warnings, and drive themselves into nervous breakdowns. This type fills the sanatoriums seeking diets and rest cures. Leo rules the heart, spine and generative organs. It can easily be seen that a sudden end can be the result of unrestrained Leo desires.

Mars is very powerful in Leo, and this influence brings (as in Aries) rashness and a susceptibility to accidents. Since Leo people love life more than some of the other Zodiacal types, it might be advisable to use temperance in physical habits, and control all rash inclinations.

Leo women are gorgeous. Many of them are the picturesque red or golden-haired beauties of stage and screen. Even those not in the public eye are often lovely to look at, with poise and outstanding ability of some sort. They too tend toward leadership. They may shine in the business world, but the professional world, especially the theatre, offers the ideal opportunities.

The Leo woman makes a fine wife. Full of passion and fire, she is loyal, responsive, and cooperative. Her energy is boundless, capabilities legion, and her appearance always a credit to her husband. However, she is an expensive luxury, dressing extravagantly, and expecting a setting of costly jewels, furs, a fine home, and everything that makes a splendid show.

The primitive type of Leo woman has the proverbial "redheaded temper." Storms of unreasonable anger will be her family's daily portion. She never reasons, but acts wholly on the spur of the moment. In her, the fine Leo pride becomes arrogance, and her blind conceit makes her a noisy, bumptious, gadabout. Needless to add, she is always over-dressed.

The Leo lover and the Leo husband have several qualities in common. They are conventionally minded men, but whole-souled in their devotion to the beloved. They are ardent, passionate, generous, and give of themselves so completely, that the return of devotion always seems small and inadequate in comparison. This is very sad for Leo, who in consequence feels unloved and unsatisfied. If the wife, children or sweetheart of these Leo men could only realize how much emotional damage they do by unresponsiveness, they would change their attitude and give as heartily as they receive.

Virgo

August 24th—September 23rd

You are happy
when reading informative material,
gaining educational goals.
You never cease to learn,
never cease to win improvements
in your work and environment.
Happiness comes
with each step
you feel is successful,
but you go right on
toward even further steps
to help create perfection.
Happiness is never a stagnant matter
but you seek it
further on
in making new efforts.
You actually find happiness
in monotonous,
difficult work
as you keep control of its complexities.
Fame does not attract you
but you will win much praise
for capabilities and tireless effort
of diligent nature.
This will bring quiet happiness,
mental joy.

YOUR BIRTHDAY IN VIRGO

People born in the sign of Virgo, the Virgin, are a blend of two forces, not entirely harmonious. These forces are Earth and Air. Virgo is an Earth sign, ruled by Mercury, whose airy influence, intellectual as it is, does not harmonize with the humble earthy influence of the innate sign-character.

This conflict of personality blends remarkably well in the average Virgo person, who may have a great deal of intellect and a small amount of earthiness, or just the reverse.

The average Virgo person is quiet, industrious, painstaking and modest. Almost a slave to his work, the Virgo native rules those who work for him by the same exacting standards. He gives and demands "measure for measure."

Generally respected, these humble people excite no envy as they progress, partly because of the modesty of their demands, and the insignificance of their personality.

The more noble types of the Zodiac look down upon Virgo

instinctively. They are not handsome, they are not idealistic, they are not heroic, and they are not adventurous. But they are, as a rule, trustworthy, clean and decent. The influence of Mercury gives them clear-thinking, practical minds capable of the material type of intellectuality. This is not to be confused with the high quality of thought of Libra, or the abstract mathematical gymnastics of Gemini. At best, these are plain people, treating life as a placid fact. Whatever dignity of position they do arrive at, they guard jealously and keep it untarnished.

The more mental type, with the urge toward intellectual Mercury qualities, lacks none of the dependability found in the humble, earthy members of the sign.

The high type of Virgoan has a cool, self-centered intellect, with a highly developed critical sense. They have some of the Gemini brilliance, but are not nearly so restless.

They accomplish whatever they set out to do because they stick to the job, no matter how lengthy and tiresome. In this way Virgo people succeed far beyond the expectations of all who know them. Many of the more distinguished Zodiacal types who appear to inherit the earth disdain to exert the effort put forth by the average Virgo person. Virgo natives, on the other hand, are willing to humbly advance their lot, and court success by work and service.

All of the Virgo processes of thought are factual, earthbound and material. Their intellectual work is always along the lines of concrete, known facts and known quantities. They cannot understand, and do not credit, flights of fancy or remote intellectual speculation. Spiritually, they respect religion as an institution of respectability. They themselves are not religious in the spiritual sense of the word. They have no desire to plumb the mysteries of life, and no understanding of involved spiritual thought. They go to church because their world would think ill of them if they did not. These people conform to recognized patterns of conduct because they are limited and fearful in spirit. They never forget the sorry consequences of misdeeds in this world rather than in the next.

The same quality of thought makes Virgo people chaste and passionless. As sweethearts and lovers they are engaging and attentive enough, but as husbands and wives they are uninspiring and passionless. In fact, where marriage is involved they are so fussy, discriminating and critical that it is hard for them to make a final choice. Frequently they do not make one at all, and many Virgo people choose to be spinsters and bachelors. It is hard for them to surrender self, and they do not know how to give unrestrainedly, or even comprehend the heights of poetic physical love. They are exceedingly cold.

When they do marry, they make kind, cooperative partners, domestic and reliable provided the pair have more of a brother and sister relationship. Even if the marriage does not begin with this plan in view, Virgoans will inspire the household with the virginal quality of thought.

Virgo faults are like their virtues, sober, grave and prosaic. The exception is the negative Virgo type, quite rare, and this is the criminal who resorts to poison.

Generally, negative Virgo people are tedious, hair-splitting, fussy, penny-pinching and boring to exasperation. When they attain any position at all, they become snobbish. Ill health is a bogey-man with Virgoans, and they dramatize their illnesses whether real or imaginary. This is the only flight of fancy Virgo people seem to understand.

As a matter of fact, Virgo natives enjoy surprisingly good health. Being temperate people, they live sensibly, and the result is usually a long life and a healthful old age. Virgo is one of the old-age signs of the Zodiac. It is to be remembered that Virgo is the health sign. Virgo rules the bowels, solar-plexus, and especially the alimentary canal.

In appearance Virgo people fall into two types, the typically "earth sign type," and the "mental Mercury type." The earth-sign type is homely, with a head far too large for the body. The body is strong and healthy, but ungraceful and badly proportioned. Knock-knees, bow-legs, and shoulders of uneven height are often found in the Virgo physique. Coloring and features are nondescript. The nose, frequently the outstanding feature in the Virgo face, is unshapely, very broad and primitive in type.

The higher type of Virgo person is somewhat better formed, with a neater figure, and smaller, more precise features.

The plain durability of the Virgo appearance suggests the life work and methods of livelihood for which these people are best suited. The high type Virgoan makes a good statistician, efficiency expert, tutor, teacher, agent for estates, broker (within limits), and lawyer for collections, contracts and wills. The less developed types make good routine civil service workers, especially in the health and investigation departments.

Women born in the sign of Virgo are as precise, hardworking and trustworthy as their brothers in the sign. They are very satisfactory as clerical workers, housekeepers, seamstresses and buyers of foodstuffs.

Libra

September 24th—October 23rd

You enjoy using artistic talents
or talking about art
with people
who are in the know.
Advanced ideas please you
and good conversation about them
makes you happy.
When beauty and harmony
are strongly in evidence in your environment,
you glow with a happy light.
You love being consulted
on matters
and may often settle disputes among friends
very amicably.
You need love
and a lifemate
who brings you
into practical use of your talents;
otherwise you might dream
and be too inactive.
Real happiness is achieved finally
by active work
and results that are admired.
Never bury
or hide your talents.

YOUR BIRTHDAY IN LIBRA

Libra, symbolized by the scales, is the sign of marriage and partnership. It might be said of the Libra people that they are the most fitted for partnership of any sign in the Zodiac. Librans are balanced, serene, temperate, intellectual, analytical and harmonious.

Like Gemini and Aquarius, Libra is an air sign, but it differs from both of these signs in many ways. The air signs indicate a high type of mentality, but Libra people have the most artistic, aristocratic and social mind of all three.

Libra is ruled by Venus, and in both appearance and temperament Librans show the highest Venusian qualities.

They are unusually delicate, refined looking people, with medium-sized, graceful figures, very regular features and small hands and feet. Everything about them, hair, eyes and complexion appears well cared for and in good health. This is somewhat deceiving as they are not at all vigorous people. They have a good physical structure and generally enjoy sound health, but they have little resistance and yield to illness if they are exposed in any way. They recover quickly, and seem to have, for such delicate constitutions, plenty of resilience.

Socially, Libra people are in great demand. They have such a highly developed sense of fitness that people learn to look to them to make decisions, for they do and say just the right thing at the right moment. Their conversation flows along easily, and they are so instinctively well-bred that society believes them to be as cool and unruffled as they appear to be.

In some respects this is true of Libra. They have great mental detachment but are the most passionate people of all the Zodiacal types. This statement might bear some modification as the sign of Scorpio has more intensity in its passion, and the Leo passions have more fire. But behind the poised front of Libra there is usually a physical nature so alive, and sensuous, and sensual, so avid for fulfillment that it is hard to believe that two forces can harmonize so completely the force of mind and the appetites of the body.

As sweethearts and lovers these people are utterly charming, partly because of their own engaging temperament, coupled with their delight at all physical union. They are not constant in their devotion, but they make changes in the affections so tactfully that the dispossessed is not always aware of the painful operation until it is all over.

In the weak Libra type this devotion to the senses sometimes gets the upper hand. They resort to extremes in sex, and do many things gracefully that would be obnoxious in other personalities. In men of this sign, the physical balance can totter and lean to homosexuality. Weak Libra women, physically lax, with a desire for luxury that overrules the moral stamina, sometimes become prostitutes.

It must always be remembered that these tendencies do not appear in the positive type who, aside from a normal desire to flirt and enjoy popularity, behave throughout the life even better than other Zodiacal divisions.

Domestically the Libra man and woman fit into the scheme of marriage. They have so much charm that they usually marry early in life. Traditionally conventional, they always preserve the home. Librans seldom seek divorce, but they do seek change. They are as gracious and well bred in the home as they are in social life, but they are difficult partners to live up to. Their own behavior so nears the ideal in outward human conduct that the marriage partner has a hard time living up to it. The other partner may be a wonderful person but entirely without the Libra ability to adjust himself so smoothly to the pace of life.

In business, Libra persons make ideal partners. They are the balance wheel of a combination, and they excel in matters of judgment, analysis, and instinctive reasoning. They seem to be somewhat conservative. This is not unprogressive, but rather an innate desire to be safe and protect the other fellow against losses that might result from the untried.

Libra people have a high type of intellect. They can comprehend any subject, up to the most involved philosophical argument. They can analyze, explain, and pass judgment on all sorts of difficulties with complete detachment.

This makes the highest group of Libran suitable for diplomacy, judgeships and international law.

As Venus rules this sign, her sway gives Libra people the taste and ability to select beautiful things. Houses, furnishings, ornaments and paintings, or decorations and design in all of the branches are suitable professions for Libra. Among the more physical Librans, dancing and modeling clothes are very suitable occupations.

Every sign has its seamy side, and the delightful Librans degenerate even as all the others. The negative Libran is spineless, lacking direction and purpose. They are often accomplished liars, using the Libra glibness for misrepresentation and willful deceit. This type of Libran can fritter away a lifetime in self-indulgence, pretense and lying. They go about with the air of fallen grandees who are far too rare for this base world. They themselves end up by almost believing the airy fabric of their dreams, and the conscious lying and trickery that are part of this personality.

Scorpio

October 24th—November 24th

You are
quite a force in the world,
bring splendid skills and mentality
to all you do.
You are a worker,
happy when busy
with worthwhile tasks.
You like to feel
a sense of power
over everything in your environment
and this means
you must get the confidence of others.
Working alone
behind the scenes
pleases you
but to win greatest happiness
you should aim for
coming out a little more with personality
and results of endeavor.
You are intense when in love
and emotional gratification
is your highest form of happiness.
Winning affluence
through use of your unequaled financial wisdom
is a challenge
that also makes you intensely happy.

YOUR BIRTHDAY IN SCORPIO

The Scorpion is the symbol of this sign and suggests itself in the disposition and character of Scorpio natives. These people are extremists in every way. They are the most dominant, ruthless, self-willed and autocratic of any Zodiacal type. They are passionate and rebellious, tearing down the tenets of God and Man alike to suit their purpose. They WILL RULE, not with the gracious majesty of Leo, or even the sharper authority of Aries, but with the fierce tyranny of a Czar. It is THEIR WAY or no way.

The enigma of all who understand the Scorpio temperament is this combination of violent qualities with a fine constructive mind. These people have a true comprehension of life, its difficulties, and problems. They are exceedingly astute, and know how to win out in the difficult battle of life. For to them everything is a battle. Yet with all that superior knowledge, they seldom take the easy way to accomplish anything, but always choose the road of contention and strife. They are contrary and contradictory, and choose to go in opposition to even their own conceptions, if it suits their mood of the moment. This sign was once called the negative side of Mars and Mars was appointed its ruler, but the newest astrological thought has described Pluto, named for the dark lord of the underworld, as the rightful ruler of the sign.

Such a picture of active unpleasantness leads one to wonder how Scorpio natives conform to this world at all. Actually they are often very successful people, of great ability, and high accomplishment.

The sign of Scorpio, ruled over by Pluto, is the sign of death, birth and the principle of sex. It also deals with problems of race preservation, reform and regeneration. The turgid passions of hatred, revenge and rivalry are also part of the Scorpio sign-personality.

In appearance the Scorpio man is thick set, even squat. He is a giant in strength, and moves with effortless power, and works with tireless energy. The face is heavy, dark and often sneering or saturnine in expression. The jaw protrudes and the mouth is determined, harsh and somewhat coarse.

The Scorpio woman is more agreeably shaped, although big boned and somewhat heavy. Sometimes the figure is grandly voluptuous. The face is generally a full oval and the mouth sensual, though not without beauty and appeal.

Both sexes are exceedingly passionate, but very often their physical capabilities are not up to the desires of the mind. Unless there is a little prudence somewhere in the make-up, the Scorpio passions can become degrading. Illness and incapacity have come to many Scorpio natives as a result of their own unreasoning sexual activities.

In the intellectual fields Scorpio people are successful as they are able to grasp and master any subject. Will power and the unconquerable desire to dominate often force them to tackle jobs that others would avoid. Usually they succeed in their work, for they are thorough, systematic and very capable. They work tirelessly for the salvation of the race, and often thanklessly, as the Scorpio personality invites quarrels, criticisms, and tumult. Working in the medical and surgical field, operating, searching for causes and cures, the Scorpio native plods tirelessly, spreading violent emotions in his wake, sometimes worship, more often hatred, but never indifference. They work and get results long after other types have ceased their efforts.

Scorpio people are philosophical, for they are deeply analytical and profound. But, unable to separate their discoveries from their own temperament, they color everything with a dark, pessimistic shroud, even when their common sense and experience have taught them that the facts are different. They are impossible in argument, as only they can win.

At the head of a great project, this type of inflexible command has its value, and though the big boss (if he is Scorpio) may be well hated, he is also obeyed. Work carried on under such direction is never shallow, but always well done and permanent, as if it were created to fight the elements. It is quite usual to find a Scorpio man with all his faults at the head of a vast undertaking.

Scorpio people are often engaged in the execution of great wills, and the settlement of big inheritances. The high type of the sign are scrupulously honest, and have pathological interest in bereavement that makes them zealous in completing settlements and in making a material return as far as it is possible for spiritual losses.

They are prolific people in every way, and they are prodigious workers. They like large families, even though they make the poorest parents, being tyrannical, overly possessive and violent. But, despite their unsuitability of temperament, the principle of sex operates more fully with Scorpio than any other type in the Zodiac. They have large families.

By the same token, Scorpio is temperamentally unfit for matrimony, and though almost always married, the Scorpio husband is violent, too demanding, jealous, suspicious, and over-bearing.

The Scorpio wife may be a shrew, keeping her family in a state of nervous exhaustion with her tyranny and temper. For Scorpio, success in marriage comes when the type is slightly modified by the moon, ascendant, or some other planet, powerful in the birth chart. Or marital success may come when the opposite partner is yielding and very docile, and even stimulated by such explosive guidance. As friends, Scorpio people succeed rather better, but when intimacies grow too close, conflict arises.

Thus in all human relations Scorpio revolts. The mind is large, able, capable and comprehensive, but natives make life a bitter struggle, tinctured with their own warped brand of humor and relieved by secret lust.

The Scorpio people have just had some strong planetary stresses and probably are wondering how long they will be singled out for extra activity. Some of the hectic short-term action may slow down; but slow moving planets are in angles for Scorpio natives, and will continue in those positions for some years.

Sagittarius

November 23rd—December 21st

You are happy
in mental encounters
with others,
in discussing high issues
and ideas you feel stimulating.
Your enthusiasms take you
hither and yon
and you enjoy the changes and variety
that thus spice your life.
To be socially popular,
attend glittering affairs
delights you.
Impulsive travel pleases
and you often just throw a few things
into a traveling case
and leave for some point
that interests you suddenly.
Your work must be happy,
that means
variety and challenge to your ingenuity
must be involved.
You love adventure
and all new personal contacts
give you a sense
of starting an adventure
as does romance.

YOUR BIRTHDAY IN SAGITTARIUS

The sign of Sagittarius is symbolized by the centaur, half horse, half man, drawing a bow from which an arrow is about to dart.

It is a beautiful sign, promising the native a high type of mind and noble impulses.

Physically, Sagittarians are distinguished looking people, tall, well-developed and athletic. Our mental picture of the classic hunter as well as the modern athlete is a good conception of what the Sagittarian looks like. This grace of figure is largely a part of the early youth, for Sagittarians have a zest for good living, and by the time these people have reached years of discretion, the body is mature in outline and some-what corpulent. All through the life they present a very fine appearance.

The Sagittarians take an active interest in sports and out-door activities from their earliest youth upward. They have, however, a great sense of fitness, and the sports of their youth are often laid aside as time advances for amusement suitable to the age of the native.

Sagittarian women are the "Diana type." They are usually tall, often auburn-haired, and what we moderns have learned to describe as "stunning."

The expression in both sexes is apt to be vivacious, laughing and sunny. The mien is cultured, and the features themselves medium-sized, clear and well formed. Few sign characters start life with so many advantages.

The health of the Sagittarian is good. They have naturally sound bodies, but delicate nervous systems. They have a tremendous enthusiasm for life, and are not at all self-centered. The result is too often over-strain and too much activity, mental or physical. Exposure and risk make them, as a group, subject to sudden illnesses. Sagittarians have almost as many accidents as the Aries people, because of their enthusiastic energy, and self-forgetfulness. These people are an easy prey for fevers, for they drive themselves to the peak of activity and continue to work long after another person would have recognized the signs of illness and quit. They suffer from nervous indigestion and run a temperature under almost any strain. Sagittarius rules the hips and thighs, and during the early youth the limbs are in danger of sudden accident. Later in life, high blood pressure, rheumatism and sciatica are possible. Oddly enough, despite the many susceptibilities of this sign, it is one of the old age signs of the Zodiac.

It is as if the love of these people for life itself and the urge to see what happens in the world, communicates itself to Nature, who preserves them here far beyond the normal span.

The Sagittarian intellect is of a very high quality. Their mind far surpasses the cold functions of Gemini, the abstract estheticism of Libra, or the soaring idealism of Aries. The Sagittarian mind is mature, farseeing, and practically imaginative. They have the kind of vision that understands the world and loves it for what it is, and not for what it ought to be.

Sagittarians are very broad-minded, tolerant, humorous, and truthful. They are big hearted, understanding, and entirely lacking in malice or petty jealousies.

In disposition they are jovial, in manner cordial. Their passions are healthy, spontaneous and without inhibition.

In speech they are very frank and outspoken, stating their likes and dislikes rather too freely. Despite their philosophical outlook, they have many prejudices, and even hatreds. They discuss their feelings loudly, and are very fluent and colorful in expression.

If we examine the symbol of the sign, and notice the type of the man who is part horse, it is plain that he is not a youth. Maturity and success do not come early to the Sagittarian. The very qualities for which the sign is distinguished—philosophy, religion, guidance in the life, and magnificent exploit—are naturally the work of age and experience. Sagittarians fulfill their mission as great thinkers and teachers in every walk of life.

Naturally we do not find a Jovian philosopher in every Sagittarian, nor was that the case in the olden days when Socrates flourished. But we do find many of these fine qualities alive in all Sagittarians.

They have always made wonderful teachers, writers and journalists. They are particularly well equipped to be lecturers and public speakers.

The sign governs world commerce and far-flung enterprise. Many Sagittarians are princes of commerce, and great financiers.

They are splendid politicians, and make great clergymen. For both of these professions, widely separated as they are, the Sagittarian has the ideal qualities of vision, practical power, and human sympathy.

Sometimes the Sagittarian is too much of a philosopher for modern organized religion. He is apt to question accepted

religious theories, and many religious assumptions he refuses to regard as facts.

Domestically the Sagittarian is not always a success. His
interests are too diffused. The whole world interests these
people so much that it is hard for them to confine their
thoughts and affections to one personal taste. They do not
value personal, possessive love as highly as universal love.
They are not jealous, and will not endure the supervision
of domestic life. Too often they decide to change partners
when they are married, and frequently are engaged to be
married more than once in early youth. It is not so much
that they tire of the opposite sex, as that the whole scheme
of romantic love is to them a rather youthful diversion, in-
vested by our world with more seriousness than the Sagittarian nature can accord to it.

Since all of the sign-characters have their negative type,
Sagittarius is no exception to the rule.

Low-grade Sagittarians are boastful and bragging. There
is no limit to the variety and color of the lies that they can
invent. When they are promoting illicit schemes, no story
is too fantastic for public consumption. This type is the
"Get-rich-quick Wallingford" of the Zodiac, and will take
advantage of anyone for the sheer practice of "keeping his
hand in." They will promise you the world, with no inten-
tion of keeping a fraction of the promise. They are flatter-
ers, always ready with the empty compliment. No other type
can soar so high, and fall so low. The negative Sagittarian
is a complete four-flusher.

Capricorn

December 22nd—January 19th

Rewards you receive
from ardent effort
make you happy.
You like to show
unusual capacity
for work of worthwhile type.
Building up a business of your own
can be the epitome of happiness for you.
You like to feel you are in charge,
a person of authority.
Some lust for rulership is here
and you can be happy
when you know
you do control others
and have their esteem.
You may be
an ardent worker
for community improvement,
giving your concern to public matters
and being recognized for your value
' brings happiness.
A family
of which you can be proud
is another source of joy.
Opportunities to win affluence
make you happy
and are not lost
for you seize them quickly.

YOUR BIRTHDAY IN CAPRICORN

The sign of Capricorn has no graces. The native is rather like one of those royal babies of old who were neglected in the cradle by all twelve of the fairy godmothers. However, the sign is seldom found unmodified, and much of the severity is softened by the influence of other planets.

In the pure state, the type is austere, super-critical, fault-finding and overbearing. They are dissatisfied, no matter what the recompense. They can find something to criticize in everyone else, although they view their own accomplishments as almost perfect.

Even the appearance of the pure Capricorn type is unprepossessing. They are bony, angular, and spare of figure. The bones are large, and the physique, although very healthy, has an ill-assorted look, as if some clumsy hand had fitted the limbs together. The expression is dour, Saturnine, and seldom relieved by spontaneous laughter. The coloring is very dark, and the whole personality pervaded by a shade of melancholy.

These people do not realize the depressing effect that they have upon others. They think of themselves as exceedingly accomplished, and much above their associates. They think that their eternal criticism is superior discernment, and that no one measures up to their own standards. In their secret hearts, bosses, friends and relatives are greatly beneath them, and they constantly pity themselves for being thus afflicted with the small minds around them.

Actually their mental equipment is good, and they have a vigorous intellect well able to help them succeed in business. They have a fine comprehension of how to do business in the serious, less imaginative, routine way. Instinctively they realize that they have no capacity for the inventive, the new or the original, and they seek to belittle these qualities in others, by exalting routine, and exaggerating the virtues of the true and tried. Because of the general skepticism where innovations are concerned their conservatism often wins out over the ideas of better men. They are quick to seize an advantage, as fair play is not one of their virtues.

The Capricorn native is a useful person in business, despite the aforementioned faults. He can be depended upon to follow his routine and complete his tasks with enviable exactitude. His attendance is perfect and he never misses any of his duties. If in charge of investments, provided the account is directed, he will carry out instructions to the letter. Money is never misappropriated, and a fine satisfactory account is rendered whenever called for. The Capricorn financial judgment is apt to be too conservative for real profits. Natives are miserly people by instinct, and cannot relax this tendency even when paid to make money for someone else.

No matter what field of endeavor they adopt for the life work, it is always taken with great seriousness. Nothing is ever light or trifling to these people, and the smallest tasks in their hands assume great importance.

They are exceedingly ambitious people and think of the

highest positions as theirs by right. It is remarkable that with such a stilted type of ability they can go through life always believing that the best should be theirs, but the Capricorn self-confidence is only equaled by selfishness.

While they are pursuing their course, bent upon attaining their ends, they can exist on less money than any other type of personality. The mountain goat, symbol of the sign, lives a hazardous existence on a few dry twigs, while the only home it knows is a series of uneven crags that it clings to, sure-footed and confident. This is an accurate description of the Capricorn native's struggle for existence, and his method of meeting the problem. He can adjust himself to any hardship to attain an end. His nature repels luxury or even the average pleasures and social contacts so necessary to the well-being of other Zodiacal types.

Capricorn people seek no friends, as they distrust almost everyone, and are so old for their age, whatever it happens to be, that it is hard to know into what group they rightfully belong.

They do not avoid marriage, however, but accept it as part of our inherited scheme of life. They are passionate and demanding in home life, getting a great deal of attention and respect in view of the dullness of their company and the lack of inspiration in everything that they have to offer. Indeed, it is seldom that they offer anything, but they expect instant obedience from their children, and enthusiastic affection from their wives. They distrust everyone in their home, and are always suspiciously investigating to see if they can uncover some disloyalty directed against them. It may be that instinctively and secretly they realize their shortcomings, and judge accordingly that such poverty of temperament cannot expect true devotion. Regardless of all this, their homes are seldom broken up, and all the conditions of severity and servitude that they exact of others are more often than not cheerfully fulfilled. The Capricorn parent of either sex is a type often commented on by other parents.

"You see," they say, "the less you do for children, the more they do for you."

The Capricorn woman is seldom very different from the man. Fortunately this sign blends with other aspects in forming a personality, even more completely than the other signs, and the natural harshness of the type is softened. A little of the Capricorn influence is admirable, adding stability, honesty and thoroughness to the character. When the predominating force is softly feminine, the stamina of Capricorn is a great virtue.

Aquarius

January 20th—February 18th

You are happiest
when needed by others
and being successful
with helping them.
You like to sponsor
causes for freedom and equality,
help make it possible for all people
to know the good things of life.
A career
in which you can alleviate bad conditions
will make you happy.
You love to study
in philosophical regions or occult lore.
You are an idealist
with large dreams
but find happiness
only when you can
make them come true
at least to some extent.
When friends
or a loved one
share your interests
and good discussion takes place,
you are in your element for joy.
Creative work makes you happy,
attaining ideals is a goal.

YOUR BIRTHDAY IN AQUARIUS

People born in this sign of the Zodiac cannot be judged by the standards that measure other people. This is perhaps the one completely unselfish type, in whose motives for behavior and in whose impulses may be seen a divine touch.

Aquarian people love humanity, not as the Sagittarian does, in a human way, with all its faults, but rather they love the life principle. To the Aquarian, the fact that there is life makes all things possible. He sees in mankind an exalted future, where a universal harmony is the natural scheme. To the Aquarian, world peace, arising out of the highest qualities of men is the ultimate goal.

Aquarians see good in everything. They manage to get along with everyone and seldom find fault with any person or condition no matter how unjustly they may suffer from it. They are not martyrs, however, and if they are imposed upon, they will extricate themselves so adroitly that the real culprit is always mysteriously revealed.

In appearance Aquarians are usually pleasant-looking people. It is as if some of the rare qualities of their mind were translated into a visual form. Aquarians have graceful medium sized figures. The head is very well shaped, with a broad benevolent brow and a generally sympathetic expression. They look, and are, exceedingly fit and healthy. This is partly due to the fact that they are so sensible about health habits that disease seldom gets a chance to attack them. They guide their lives into paths of industry, and keep busily occupied with some useful work.

Whatever the work of Aquarians, it must always have a touch of culture and idealism. They never choose an uninteresting job as a life work, and whatever it is, they invest it with new life and an individual slant that is often productive of great financial returns.

Not that the Aquarian loves money for itself, as does the Capricornian, but rather he loves it for what it can buy in the way of progress and development for the work that he is doing. For, be assured, this type is always working, and hard work agrees with them. They can accomplish a great deal in very little time, and with half the energy that most people put into a task. They are naturally able people, and inject into almost any task some improvement in method.

It must be remembered that the sign of Aquarius is ruled by Uranus, the planet of upheaval, revolution and change. The qualities of Uranus are strong in the Aquarian character, but they are not, as they suggest, unpleasantly aggressive. When the word revolution is mentioned, the natural reaction is one of uncertainty or even fear. Aquarians have it in their make-up to change any condition in the life that appears to them unhealthy or lacking in progress. They always aim for the highest in human harmony, and anything less causes them acute unhappiness. But this Uranian tendency toward change is seldom accompanied by the horrors usually connected with revolution, that is unless other conditions are at work.

In their relations to friends, business associates, and loved ones, Aquarians are at their best. They enjoy human contacts and are most social, friendly people. They love to entertain, and frequently collect all kinds of queer people under their roof. This sometimes has bad results. They are inclined to trust everyone, and seldom doubt a hard-luck story. The result is that they are often deceived, and suffer consequent losses. This is never a lesson to them, as they consider humanity a study. They are always anxious to observe human conduct under all kinds of conditions. To the Aquarian, a person is never entirely bad, even when he commits wicked actions.

Aquarians make the best friends of any of the Zodiacal types. They are willing to give a great deal of themselves, and usually receive a great deal in return. Their friendship is appreciated by all those who have the privilege of this enjoyment. In addition, friendship with an Aquarian, as well as love, has an inspiring quality that helps to raise every relationship to its highest form.

In matters of romance and love, the Aquarian is more satisfactory than the Sagittarian, but he does share some of the same preference for universal love over personal love. However, when the Aquarian chooses a love, it is usually with great discrimination. In that field he is not easy to please, and responds only to the rarest type of passion and the cleanest personality. Usually Aquarians look for some mutual mental interest in the loved one. When they do find an intellectual companion who appeals in a fine way to their senses, they are faithful forever.

In all matters of human conduct, the Aquarian may be said to be the most nearly above reproach than any other Zodiacal type.

They seldom diverge from type, and the action of other planets has less effect on the basic character than any of the other signs. As usual, there is a negative type. These people are somewhat dangerous, for they have a good many of the likable qualities of the major Aquarian, but none of his constructive ability. They stir up conditions of discontent and dissatisfaction in their environment, and with many assurances that all will be well, they proceed to let the chips fall where they may, for they have no ability to adjust matters.

These natives are often glib talkers. They can talk themselves into good jobs, and then proceed to hold the job by fooling the boss. The fact that they are incapable is usually revealed by some accident. A low-grade Aquarian can make so much trouble by his nosiness, interference, and upsetting point of view that it takes the combined efforts of a good many different personalities to undo the confusion created by the original conflagration.

Aquarians love a hobby, and it is usually a useful one. They frequently take a great interest in advanced theories and in the schools for education along special lines. They want to bring luxury and privilege to every person, but they also want that person to have the intellectual background to understand and appreciate great and good things. It is true that they have deep sympathy for poverty, but they have a deeper concern for ignorance. Aquarians wish to raise the mental standard of the whole world before anything is done about physical salvage for the masses. To the Aquarian mind it is more important to make a man think than eat. Perhaps instinctively the Aquarian knows that somehow man will eat, but he must be trained to love to think. Aquarians believe that only when all men are responsible mentally will true happiness prevail.

Pisces

February 19th—March 20th

You like
the quiet happiness
of knowing
you are loved and understood.
You need to be appreciated
and your emotions
must be treated with great sympathy.
You also like
to advance the lot of others,
bringing more justice to the world
pleases you,
and if you can
work in medical fields
to relieve suffering
you will know
great happiness.
Giving your attention to the underprivileged
can make you happy.
You must find friends
who share your interests in expansive causes
and are cheerfully active
to bring about better conditions.
Developing an artistic skill
can bring new happiness;
if you haven't done this
it is time to take such a step.

YOUR BIRTHDAY IN PISCES

People born in the sign of Pisces are a puzzle to everyone, as well as to themselves. The symbol of the sign, two fishes swimming in opposite directions, typifies the contradictions in the nature of the Piscean.

Neptune rules the sign, and creates in the natives a dreamy, responsive, impressionable, sensitive spirit, without any ability to cope with the realistic conditions of daily life. Neptune himself comes to us as a gay, cheerful, jovial, laughing personality, but in the legends of antiquity he is always the arch-deceiver and trickster.

Pisceans have all of these qualities. They are amiable, sweet-tempered people, very socially inclined, and exceedingly likable. But their character lacks direction to such an extent that they themselves do not really know what it is they want. Their sympathy is boundless. If illness is mentioned in their presence, they are a bundle of aches and pains. They know exactly how everyone feels, with more intensity than the person with the pain.

Venus and the Moon are very powerful in Pisces, but these planets in this sign only make the native self-indulgent and more moody and whimsical. It is easy to see how the sign influences tend to rob the native of the stamina needed to fight the realities of life.

This combination of planets governing the sign character gives the high type Piscean all of the qualities already mentioned, with the addition of a really exalted imagination, in which the native retreats to escape from the harsh world.

This spiritual departure sometimes results in the beautiful 'creative work of poetry, music, and painting. Sometimes the Piscean visions are followed by a real attempt to visualize the natives' schemes for the betterment of mankind. They see so clearly the ills of the world, and plan in their imagination so many ways to alleviate the suffering of mankind that it is too bad that more Piscesns have not the power to make these schemes a reality. Sometimes this is accomplished, and the world benefits from a sincere plan for its welfare. But more often the Piscean dreams away the time in fretful discontent.

Even the high type of this sign is intensely sorry for himself (or herself). He considers that his involved spiritual theories make him superior to the world around him, and the native seldom realizes that his way of life is most deceptive. These people cannot be depended upon from one moment to the next, and the expression of their thoughts changes with their audience. They consider themselves the personification of truth, while in reality the devious quality of their minds and their complicated desires, (often dark and questionable), make them the most untruthful of all of the Zodiacal types. To the Piscean, telling untruths is part of his own code of self-deception. When faced with his falsehoods, he always has a glib explanation, very ethical in expression, that turns a tide of sympathy on himself. A Piscean will never admit that he is capable of a dishonest or unethical act. They set a high value on right thinking, and will tell any sort of story to prove that they of all people would never do a wilfully wrong act.

This is a very difficult type of character to cope with in the life, for Pisceans excite, in one way or another, the sympathy of almost every one they contact. The person who uncovers deceit in a Piscean is enmeshed in a net of explanation meant to destroy the truth of the situation and recover esteem and sympathy for the native.

These people love the unknown and mysterious. They are devoted to studies of the occult, spiritualistic, and esoteric fields of imagination. They believe in the truth of these phantom worlds, and however unconvincing the physical manifestations may be to the other Zodiacal types, the Pisceans believe in them.

The mixed Piscean type, with a generous bolstering of sturdy planetary influences, can use this love of the spirit to great advantage in the life. In such a case it makes the native more sensible in sympathies, and gives a more sincere spiritual balance.

With the maze of contradiction and clash of urges in the basic character, it is easy to understand how hard it is for this type to adjust themselves to the life. They are so impressionable that any theory vividly described is at once their own. Their enthusiasm for causes, platforms and phobias changes almost with the season, and they themselves are so victimized by fact and fancy, truth and falsehood, that the weaker types seldom achieves any purpose in the life.

To hear them talk, this would not seem to be the case, for they are very glib, colorful, and plausible in speech. It is only when they are unable to carry out a program expected of them that this inherent incapability is revealed.

This does not mean that all Pisceans are incapable. Quite the contrary. Among all the Signs of the Zodiac are to be found great people and successful people. But, with the Piscean type of character there must be a grouping of planets in the natal chart strong enough to offset the delusive Neptune character, and the moody dominance of the moon, and the lax, self-indulgent Venus influence. These influences in moderation are very glamorous, and do much to soften a character and make the personality more intriguing, but when there are no planets in powerful positions to add stamina, the whole is likely to suffer.

Pisces people succeed as musicians, poets, and ministers or in the healing professions. In the business world they tend toward industry connected with fluids, (because this is a water sign), travel by water, oils, beverages, chemicals, etc. They are interested in the world of illusion and gravitate toward the motion-picture field, cosmetics, costumes, etc.

The Pisces people are not robust. They have rather a weak constitution, and are so susceptible to suggestion that they can work themselves into a state where any illness is a possibility. They have little resistance and succumb to exposure. They suffer from illness so much during the life that they sometimes contract the drug habit. This does not often go so far as to become a vice, but they resort to drugs and drink alcohol more frequently than many of the other Zodiacal types.

The appearance of the Piscean varies with the placing of the other signs in the nativity. The face is usually outstanding in softness of outline and expression. All of the lines are round and gentle. The women of this sign have especially soft, insinuating, expressive faces. The sign runs to flesh, but in the women of the type, there is, especially during youth, a sensuous grace that is seductive. Many oriental beauties are of the Pisces type. Both sexes often become fat during early middle age because of overeating, overdrinking, and no exercise.

In love and marriage the Piscean is at home. Both men and women of this type love domestic life, and they are the most willing of all the Zodiacal types to carry out the romantic legend of lover and sweetheart throughout the married life.

They show great affection in the home and flatter the mate with little attentions and gestures of affection. This is very lovely when the character has some stability, but when the Piscean make-up is not mixed with the sturdier qualities, every pretty face is a temptation, and every manly figure a possible thrill. The stronger type of Piscean sublimates these wandering fancies in intellectual pursuits.

THE MOON

The moon shares importance with the sun in your horoscope in making you the kind of person you are.

Many people after reading a solar horoscope, (which is a
character analysis of a person, based on the influence and
quality of the sun in the birth sign,) complete the reading,
disappointed with the material, not because it is not good
enough, but because they do not recognize themselves.

A common response to this statement is that few people
know themselves, and that regardless of what sort of picture
is presented to the native, he or she will not recognize or
like it.

This may be true in a few isolated cases, but average persons have a deep-rooted desire to know themselves, not only the superficial front that everyone knows, but those hidden depths of the spirit that by their silent motivation really make the history of the native.

There are several reasons why the solar horoscope may never reveal this unfamiliar self. Sometimes the sun is found in a sign where it is weak, and does not give the personality the strength to mark it indelibly. The sun is notably weak in Libra and Aquarius.

In other natal figures the sun may be opposed and in that way lose some of its fiery strength.

But there are other horoscopes wherein the moon is well aspected, or the position very strong. In addition to these two facts, the moon in each one of the twelve signs makes for even more definite qualities of thought than the sun in the same sign. These qualities may be more variable, less stable, and apparently more transient, but they are intense, and will give the native a clear picture of the disposition, and the extent of rulership over the whole being by this feminine, elusive, and spiritual manifestation.

THE MOON IN ARIES

People with the moon in Aries in their birth charts have a deep, unquenchable yearning for leadership. They long for all of the material signs of power. The satisfaction of the spirit does not satisfy them, and they want to enjoy the authority and often the luxury that goes with power.

Sometimes this position makes all this possible, for the moon in Aries gives originality of thought, brilliant, flashing ideas, and a constantly changing mental picture. People with this kind of a mind can frequently turn these ideas into money or into channels that lead to the position that they are so earnestly seeking.

The moon in Aries gives the native an irritable disposition. These people are brisk and snappy, with sudden outbursts of temper followed by sharp repartee and biting comments. Words flare up in them like flames, and when angry they find themselves able to express themselves with even more gusto than when completely at ease.

People with the moon in Aries are seldom calm for any length of time. Everything that interests them excites them. They build up mental pictures of social giants that they intend to slay, and even when their impulses lead them into more everyday channels of thought and action, they dream of "more worlds to conquer."

Since the main result of the moon in this sign is to make physical conditions out of thoughts, the native has, to begin with, a very hard task. Sometimes the objective is so difficult to attain that it borders upon physical danger, and many people with the moon in Aries have been known to create conditions that ended in their own death. These people seem to have no ability to weigh or measure the proportion of their plans. Whatever the ideas they conceive and wish to fulfill, they are constructed materially without regard to consequences. Their mental energy sweeps everything before them to a conclusion, and at no time during the process are they able or willing to halt the tide.

It must not be supposed that this is an inferior position. The reactions from this luna rule and the type of mind that it controls are lofty in quality and capable of great accomplishment.

The moon has great power over the love nature, and often has a principal hand in shaping the mental responses to romantic love and the physical urge.

Posited in Aries, the moon gives the native a keen delight in the quest for love. To such a person it is a hunt, and the thrill lies in the advance, retreat, and chase. It is an artful mental game of hide-and-seek far more delightful to the hunter than the passionate fulfillment. The peak of this type of passion may be hot, but it will be very brief. When the manoeuvres of the game are exhausted, this flame of passion burns low. The demand is insistent but quickly fulfilled.

In a woman's horoscope this position tends to bring uncertainty into the love life. It gives her a somewhat masculine outlook in love matters, making her too changeable, moody, whimsical and flirtatious. This attitude has often been described as successful, especially when desirous of winning an unwilling mate. With this particular manifestation, it tends to discourage the lover, who, upon such cavalier treatment, gives up, hopeless of winning the beloved.

On the other hand, this position of the moon often tends to attract to the woman a man very like her in temperament. He will be brilliant, able, well-to-do and generous, but he will not be steadfast or faithful.

In the horoscope of a man with the moon in Aries, the love nature is apt to be subject to many ups and downs. Natives are likely to meet with all sorts of disappointments and even disillusion. This is caused not so much because the beloved is unworthy, but because this quality of mind attracts persons to the native who already have what used to be called, "a past." Too often the sweetheart of the native has lived through a tragedy of which "the melody lingers on." It will be the constant misery of the lover to face this past until he is forced through circumstances to retire from the picture.

The moon in whatever position it is found in the horoscope plays a vital part in shaping the health of the native. While it must not be supposed that the position of the moon can make one ill or well, it can establish boundaries and show inclinations.

The position of the moon at birth can point out where the weakest spot is to be, (if afflicted in the natal chart), or can show where the mighty human body will wear the thinnest.

The moon, so largely the director of the energy, will give the native a vast quantity of zest and dash, but at the least indication of excitement or trouble, he is overwhelmed. Too much disturbance will upset the entire system.

The head and face are very sensitive, and this includes the skin, bony structure, skull, hair and teeth. The eyes also belong in this group, but under Aries, the "moon is very clear sighted," and the vision is exceptionally good. The teeth too are often very strong, but they are in constant need of special care. This is caused by irregularities in structure rather than weak teeth.

This aspect of the moon often makes care of the diet a necessity. The excess of nervous energy and the hasty excitable living habits of the individual give a positive tendency toward nervous indigestion.

The special complaints of this position are neuralgia, catarrh, and impacted wisdom teeth, fevers, nervous indigestion and apoplexy.

Even though the material aims are stressed by the moon in Aries, the spiritual trends of so idealistic and soaring an urge must not be forgotten. The particular message of the spirit imparted by Luna in this position is an intense striving for concrete physical improvements in the life created out of rare thoughts, which are meant to triumph over a disappointing world.

THE MOON IN TAURUS

People with the moon in Taurus have a very practical temperament. On the surface they are stolid, and appear to be reserved, although this is not the case, but just their clever way of sizing up a situation without showing their hand.

The moon in this sign does not make them fanciful in any way, but leans rather toward an ambitious, worldly, selfish outlook that operates slowly and quietly under cover to attain personal ends. For a luna aspect, the moon in Taurus is practical and effective, so that even if the obstacles are many and the path apparently blocked, the native by sheer determination frequently arrives at the coveted goal.

That goal for these people is a luxurious home, an epicurean table, plenty of money for travel and entertainment, expensive clothes, and a large circle of admiring friends. They covet all the worldly benefits, and scheme for them in secret, always being careful to show a good-natured face to the world.

This good nature is really placidity. The natives are both unwilling and unable to show violent emotion, as they instinctively know that it will wreck their plans. They have a naturally unruffled disposition, and however moved they may be by events in the life, they are outwardly calm. In the rare cases where the natives forget this rule, the results are disastrous to themselves. They have no practice with explosive emotions, and no machinery for gauging the extent of the damage from one of their own outbursts. When they do forget themselves, their cause is usually lost.

All this may indicate that these people take life easily. This is not so. Their difficulties are legion. They are not intellectual, and while they have a very practical, astute, shrewd ability to judge the average conditions presented by life, people with such lofty ambitions need plenty of mental equipment to fight their way to the top. They do not have the intellectual mind, but a sort of sly instinct serves them in place of it.

It may be argued that no base or ordinary qualities of the mind can take the place of the lofty, but where the goal is largely material success, the lunar Taureans leave no stone unturned to make their mental make-up take care of them.

In many instances, "luck" is part of the luna force in power here, and this position brings with it gifts, bequests, legacies, property and many of the material luxuries demanded of life by this planetary position. It is to be seen that fulfillment is a part of the temperament here described, and one way or another, the native gets what is wanted.

The moon in Taurus gives ability of several sorts. People having this position in the natal chart make fine artists and artisans. They succeed in some of the scientific fields, principally the practical sciences. They are very capable in agricultural development and do well in trade. Their principal virtue is revealed in their method, which is painstaking, hardworking and persevering regardless of difficulties. They do not reason why, but remain faithful to their objective.

The love nature of both the men and women having this position in the birth horoscope is sensuous, self-seeking, and demanding. They are apt to experience sentimental, romantic love affairs in the life, and invariably end a courtship with marriage.

Women with this lunation in the chart often make rich marriages to men considerably higher in the social scale than themselves. They get a great deal of adulation, and seem to gravitate toward the type of husband who takes his responsibilities as a mate very seriously. These women are sheltered and protected all through the life, although the scale of wealth surrounding them sometimes rises and falls.

The men who have the moon in Taurus in their natal chart love with great depth and intensity, but are inspired to select women of vast ambition and an equally prodigious

appetite for spending. These men are frequently driven to
the limit of their strength to provide the type of home that
the lady of his choice has become accustomed to. Frequently
this urge arouses all of his dormant ability, and he succeeds.
Sometimes he is less fortunate, and suffers greatly in the
struggle.

The moon in Taurus gives the same amount of protective
stamina against disease as does the sun in Taurus. Both of
these great rulers, unless afflicted, will give the native great
strength of body, and tremendous endurance.

The moon well aspected in the natal chart might even indicate a very long life, although the sun in a similar position
has much the same meaning.

Although this is a position of vigor and virility, the native
does not recover from an illness quickly or easily. Once
stricken, the disease takes such a strong hold on the system
that the chances of recovery are weaker than might be expected. Many of the less robust types recover quickly from
a complaint that would undo a person receiving this luna
aspect.

The diseases most to be guarded against when the moon is
posited in Taurus are principally throat troubles, minor and
major. Sore throat and tonsillitis, of course, stiff neck, ear-
ache, and disturbances of the thyroid gland; also lock jaw,
laryngitis, and swollen palate.

This position when afflicted brings a leaning toward goiter,
abscesses, quinsy sore throat, diphtheria and gangrene. However, people with the moon in Taurus, even when afflicted,
must have a planetary clash of great violence or the action
of a malefic, to produce conditions of the above description.

THE MOON IN GEMINI

The moon posited in Gemini in the natal figure gives a
purely intellectual urge.

Gemini is an air sign, and the character that the moon
disperses from this position is light, airy, mercurial and bril-

liant. The inclinations of the native receiving this lunation are intellectual but cold.

These people incline toward abstract thought, and have an avid thirst for knowledge. No subject is too obscure for their interest and it always appears that they are packed with information. This is not always true, as the Moon in Gemini does not give a very thorough disposition to the native, and while their desire for knowledge is intense, they do not study their interests deeply enough to really digest the subjects.

The truth of the matter is that these natives are mentally brilliant, with naturally acute perceptions, and any study that catches their momentary interest becomes clear and lucid at once. They appear to have grasped the whole gamut of the subject, but if a detailed examination were given, much would be found wanting. However the intellect is very active, though somewhat unsympathetic, loving knowledge impersonally, and devouring it with an avid mental curiosity. The human side of any intellectual problem makes it neither more nor less interesting.

Despite this unsympathetic picture of the "Moon in Gemini disposition," the native is apt to be popular in the social world as this influence makes people quick-witted, exceedingly humorous, apparently very well informed, with the most attractive, graceful mannerisms, and fluent, amusing conversation. If they are callous, rather shallow, and cold, the average person is seldom aware of it, and only enjoys the agreeable society offered by the chance meeting.

Actually the moon posited in Gemini is a weak position, in that the moon's influence throws off all restraint, and becomes so reflective a body that every vagrant whim of this mercurial sign is dispersed into the disposition of the native.

In a woman's horoscope this is not a very good aspect. It is true that the native will have a quick mind, scintillating wit, and often several useful talents, but she will also be extremely pleasure loving, light minded, shallow and gossiping. This leaning toward gossip can be very dangerous. The native seems never to know when to stop talking, and frequently talks herself into trouble.

Trouble is not unusual in the lives of women with this lunation. Most of it is caused by their mental state, which is highly nervous, and from the heights of joy they drop to the depths of gloom. These descents into bogs of mental depression leave the native a complete wreck.

The men having the moon in Gemini have somewhat better luck. They are often very successful as newspaper men, advertising agency writers, authors, humorists and musical comedy dramatists. They are likely to make plenty of money, and enjoy great popularity. The temperamental coldness of the type often helps them in the business world.

The same tendency to gossip endangers the social popularity of the man as well as the woman with this lunation in the birth chart. Both sexes often pay a terrible price for this tendency to talk too much.

Domestically this is rather an insecure position. Men with this figure in the birth chart are usually well placed in life, due to their earning power, and therefore able to support a wife, but they are so flirtatious, and take love so lightly, that the wife frequently finds herself neglected for the next interesting personality or pretty face.

In the chart of a woman this lunation makes her lack the domestic sense and lean entirely toward a commercial or professional life. Naturally there are times when the love nature is at a high pitch, and the struggle between the basic disposition, and the urge of the moment does not make for much harmony or happiness in the life. This type of woman, leading a very full life in public as an actress, (light comedy) or some other type always in the public eye, will have a home life that is full of depression and loneliness.

These people are not robust. They are not receptive to disease, nor do they "catch things easily," but their resistance is not very great. The physique is somewhat delicate, and the vital organs, though sound are not built for great endurance.

Since Mercury rules the hands and arms, this rulership is temporarily turned over to the Moon during her habitation of the sign. If she is afflicted, the hands and arms will be sensitive throughout the life.

The nervous system is highly delicate and must not be subjected to too great a strain. The chest and lungs are sensitive, and while neither defective or weak, must not be abused by unsound living habits. The native should not dissipate, and this means the ceaseless round of late nights, leaving no time for sufficient sleep, too much smoking, drinking, etc.

Asthma, bronchitis, pleurisy, pneumonia and tuberculosis are possible with an afflicted moon, but sensible health habits are the chief protection against illness.

Colds should never be allowed to get the upper hand of this type of physique. Illnesses do not cure themselves for these people, and in order to keep an even grade of health, they must take moderate exercise, (walking is favored) live outdoors a good deal, eat regularly of light, nourishing, wholesome foods.

This passage is not meant to imply that people with the moon posited in Gemini are weak or unhealthy. It simply means that every sign position suggests certain conditions that require moderate care in certain departments.

The Moon in Cancer

People who have the moon posited in Cancer in their natal chart express themselves through the emotions.

In this position there is nothing intellectual, active, or material. This figure in the birth horoscope makes the native the personification of the qualities that most naturally belong to the moon, regardless of sign, but since these same attributes are the major part of the Cancer influence, the urge is doubly strong.

The moon in Cancer makes people highly emotional. People with this configuration express deep love for the standard, traditional loyalties such as home, mother, country or church. They melt with tears, and boil with rage, or burn with passion according to the need of the moment. These responses are sincere and called forth by an innate veneration for established institutions.

They are sentimental, devoted, affectionate people with a gentle loving attitude toward their intimates, and a warm sympathetic feeling for humanity in general. There is a great deal of universal devotion in their attitude toward life, as if they held themselves personally responsible for all of the ills of mankind and sorrowed for every error. As strong as this feeling is, very few great healers of human ills ever come out of this group.

The emotions of this class are too personal for universal weal, but these people make ideal sons and daughters, loving parents, devoted servants, and faithful friends. It is the type of devotion that gives very loving service, and asks nothing of the beloved but to serve. This sounds like an exalted state of being, and it is both high and fine, but can be topped by the urges of Aquarian origin, which have their roots in the highest intellectual development.

The moon in Cancer makes the native very sensitive. This sensitiveness is not only a reaction to the conditions of the life, but a deliberate seeking of contact with personalities on other planes of existence. People with this figure in the chart believe instinctively that they are mediums, and constantly seek contact with the unknown or spirit world. They describe themselves as being "psychic."

Since the moon is the basis of this particular activity in the nature, it is not unusual for the emotional effects to be changeable. These natives are generally very passive, but for no special reason they will suddenly be stirred into terrific action, working madly at anything that happens at that moment to have their interest.

The same condition exists in the emotional realm. Kind and sweet-tempered as these people are, they can just as suddenly become peevish, critical, fault-finding and wholly unreasonable.

Women are of course luckier and happier with this configuration than are men. The softness of the type is more permissible in a woman, for even the world of today allows women more sentimental privileges. Besides, the hard reality of the business world is not a fit or sympathetic background for the moon in Cancer temperament. Women highly gifted in the artistic fields of poetry or the drama will find this temperament an inspiration in their work. Those other women who are purely domestic make the best of wives and mothers when they have this type of disposition in its stabler form. They look forward to domestic responsibility, and see in the routine that is so wearying to other zodiacal types only the pleasure of serving the loved ones. Sometimes this lunation takes another form of devotion, and we find some of the women with this figure in the birth chart devoting themselves to religion. They often choose to enter convents and take very strict religious vows. It is an outpouring of the same energy toward a different goal.

The men with this type of birth figure are less blessed. Modern life, (or life during any period), is always full of problems, and the struggle for existence a foregone conclusion, therefore any inherent softness in the make-up, or emotional unsteadiness, makes a man unable to carve a successful future for himself and his family. For these men always have families. They are as domestic as the women of the kind, and think of their homes before any other consideration. They make loving if somewhat exacting husbands, and spend more time in the home than the average man.

Men with this natal condition are most successful as clergymen, or in some branch of public service. Sometimes, with other assisting planetary arrangements, they can succeed in politics and on the lecture platform. They are very good pleaders, and do well at the head of reforms, causes, and campaigns for religious or social betterment. They supply the emotional appeal that is so necessary when financial help depends on the response of the public.

This figure in the birth chart does not make for a vigorous constitution. The natives are delicate, subject to a little of every kind of ailment, and never in perfectly healthy condition. They can always be said to be "ailing."

The stomach, one of their principal weaknesses, is affected not only by what they eat but by events. If the pace is exciting it upsets them, and if life is disappointing, indigestion results. All of the complications of a weak stomach belong to this type of lunation. If the moon is afflicted at birth, the complications are supposed to be dropsy, inflammatory conditions, tumors, and, in the case of women, ovarian troubles.

It must be thoroughly understood that every person with the moon posited in Cancer at birth will not be afflicted for life with the list of illnesses mentioned here. The true meaning of the passages on health indicates the tendencies of the particular configuration mentioned. These leanings are intensified when the moon is opposed by some other planet at the hour of birth. They may never develop during the life, but they point to the direction where the greatest care should be taken.

THE MOON IN LEO

This is one of the most advantageous positions in a birth horoscope for the natal moon. The moon in Leo has very little of the variable quality that makes the luna influence so vacillating in other signs. The wavering, changeable lunation giving and taking away with equal speed adds instability to most characters. But, in Leo, the moon reflects the qualities of the sign with same force that the sun shows when posited in this position.

The moon in Leo indicates a noble nature. By this is meant a person consciously choosing the good, the generous, and the honorable in his relationship to man. Natives have an instinctive urge toward rulership, equally as strong as those with the sun in Leo. They naturally come to the front in life because their disposition calmly takes command wherever they are placed. They are highly executive, and think of any duty for which they are responsible with the greatest seriousness. They revel in responsibilities, and are indefatigable workers. Usually they are most competent, and can be trusted to do the best work possible in any field that they elect.

This is never the position of small minds. Even the uneducated person with the sun in Leo has natural dignity and an instinctive comprehension of human problems. They can be trusted with the handling of other people, and are just, honest, and willing to cooperate.

People with the moon in Leo should know that life can give them a great deal if they are willing to exert themselves beyond the boundaries of their normal sphere. Some lunations are very narrow in the possibilities offered to the native, but the nature of Leo is so generous that with proper effort, more may be accomplished in the life than average success.

The dangers of this position are jealousy, vengeance, and self-sacrifice. The first point, that of jealousy, is stronger in this lunation than almost any other in the Zodiac. These natives are so jealous of their affections and possessions that they will go to any lengths to protect them from trespassers. They can be fairly consumed by jealousy so that the result is frenzied.

They are equally terrible in revenge. There is nothing subtle about their attack, and if they desire revenge they will take it openly, and with all the ferocity they can muster. Their responses to both of these passions are intense, primitive and direct.

With the moon in Leo, self-sacrifice is part of the nature. Natives give so much of themselves that they make complete dependents of those they love. This dependence brings out

the strong protective instincts in their nature, and no matter
what they have to give up for the beloved, it is yielded with
willingness. There is so much heart and passion behind
everything that they do that the objects of their devotion
must be fine indeed to live up to the heights upon which
they are placed.

The man with the moon in Leo is often very lucky in his
choice of a sweetheart or wife. It is not really luck, as these
people are very clear-sighted and able to judge character.
An inferior woman would have no appeal for this type of
man, as he is too discriminating, and his standards are too
high to allow him to choose a wife carelessly. Having made
his selection, his devotion is intense and faithful throughout
the life.

Women with the moon in Leo in the birth chart are apt
to be rather domineering and high-handed. They are just
as noble and fine as the masculine type, but the qualities
of leadership expressed in the lunation make women too
commanding. In the business world this may work out very
well, but in home life, where this type of woman gravitates,
she is too authoritative, and consequently often chooses a
weaker man than she is a woman. The possibilities are that
he will be smothered with love and care, but he may be hen-
pecked and bossed.

Both sexes are generally successful in business life, and
since their basic qualities of mind are so well developed, any
field of work or professional interest where the personality
counts and direction and executive ability can be used is
likely to be good. When there is special talent, the Leo capacity for hard work and concentration will tend toward
success.

The personal appearance of these people is outstanding.
They are usually very good-looking and dress with great care
and taste. Grooming means a lot to them, and, in the case
of the men of the type, may be one of the reasons why they
always "get their women."

And in regard to the romantic success of this position, it may be said here that this is almost the only luna position that has a purely romantic, high-minded, and spotless conception of love. By this is meant that with the moon in Leo there goes no inclination toward any form of sexual perversion or irregularity. The passions are primitive, but straight.

The health aspect for this position is robust. The natural tendencies arc toward sound basic organs, but the disposition is to overwork. With this lunation the heart cannot always stand the amount of strain it is subjected to. These people need a good deal of rest and sleep, and much simpler living habits than they by nature select. They are inclined to eat too much, and their choices of food are too elaborate for their constitution. They are also inclined to drink too much, and as life advances this often has a very bad effect on their health. With an afflicted moon, there might be a tendency to heartburn, palpitation, angina pectoris, in fact any cardiac weakness.

Illnesses likely to attack this group could, as with so many of the other lunations, be avoided by temperate health habits.

THE MOON IN VIRGO

People with the moon in Virgo have a very exacting, critical influence to deal with in the life. Everything, whether conditions of flesh or spirit, goes under the microscope of this lunation. Its people are timorous and analytical of everything without distinction of importance, and fussy with the big and little things of life. They ask for perfection in everything, and put as much time and attention into a trifling task as might go into some colossal enterprise.

They are never really pleased with anything, and no matter how fortunate a venture turns out to be, had it been completed in some other way, these people would have been better satisfied.

Life is always difficult with these natives and if it is not really so, they make this a fact by constant criticism and continual disruption of the physical environment. The home is never well kept or orderly enough for them, the cooking is atrocious, and life in general not worth living because they cannot unpack it brand-new and spotless from a hermetically sealed tin can every morning. They are cranks on every subject under the sun. Health is a "bogey" with them, and under no other lunation in the Zodiac are there influences that incline people to such extremes in taking care of the health for so little reason.

From under this load of constant irritation the Virgo man or the woman emerges, a quiet reserved being, thoughtful, intellectual in a cool, precise, unimaginative way, and very capable in the practical pursuits chosen by them as life work.

Usually they are trustworthy and honorable in a small way, and always uphold the visible standards. They are not people of vast dimensions along any lines, but the quality of the mind is, in the higher type particularly, very high. By that is meant that they are capable of succeeding in mathematical work (accountancy), scientific research, medical practice and teaching in the higher branches of learning. This does not include philosophy, but it does take in history, law, and languages, or any other study the limits of which can be defined in material terms.

This lunation does not invest the life with any of the fanciful imagery so much a part of the moon in other signs. Soberly colored by the domination of the sign Virgo, the moon makes her subject a very plain individual, full of trifling faults and many small virtues.

The love nature of both sexes under this lunation barely exists as such. They are grave, sexless people, with a cool, impersonal chastity that seems to be a part of the moon's very nature. They have no sexual curiosity, and appear to be without any real understanding as to the whole meaning of sex. They want no contact with its intimacies, or its outpouring of self. At heart they are cold, selfish people, unwilling to exert themselves outside of the casual ways of life. In the everyday gestures of living they are exceedingly active, and will put more energy into house-cleaning, attention to business, and personal doctoring than any other type of person.

Even with this inherent coldness, they are fairly popular people. The women particularly have many friends and their activities in club, or neighborhood work are constantly using every minute of their available time. If they are married, and this is often the case in spite of their temperamental dislike for intimate relationships, they make careful painstaking wives, very dutiful, but completely uninspiring. It is not unusual to find a great many spinsters with this lunation in the natal chart. These women take to business life, or rather some of the professions are favorable for them. They make good nurses, teachers, secretaries and excel in many branches of domestic science.

The men having the moon in Virgo in the natal chart are just as fussy, old-maidish and prissy as the women. In early youth they are apt to be popular with the opposite sex, largely because they are meticulous dressers, painstaking in social conduct, and very talkative when in public. They are silent enough, and serious too, when they come to have homes of their own.

This is a position of some material success. In the charts of men in particular, the qualities of perseverance, application, and flexibility of mind make it possible for them to apply themselves steadily, until they succeed. No matter what the difficulties of the task, this Virgo influence has the ability to patiently take everything in stride until the ambition is attained. Virgo people have so little personal magnetism that they are dependent for the greater part, when seeking success, upon hard work. For this, nature has given them the proper equipment.

The health indications of this position are really very good. The lunation carries with it a hardy, tough constitution, with nothing in the least delicate about it. But the mental state is a very different matter. These people are the hypochondriacs of the Zodiac. They fancy themselves heir to every ill, and since they have a natural interest in medicine, they personify themselves into patient, druggist, and doctor all rolled into one. They believe themselves able to read every prescription, and frequently diagnose their own illnesses with intense seriousness. Nine-tenths of the time these illnesses are imaginary. As has been said, they are really very healthy people, close to the soil in sturdiness, and usually live to a ripe old age.

However, when illness is their portion they have intestinal troubles. With an afflicted moon, there come disturbances of the whole digestive tract, peritonitis, anemia, appendicitis, and typhoid. Sometimes this particular figure in the natal chart leans toward strange diseases, little known and understood. It is as if the constant seeking of illness by those in this figure, occasionally, brings them to life in serious earnest.

THE MOON IN LIBRA

The moon in this position of the birth figure gives many indications of talent, and a fine intellectual capacity. The emotional nature is fluid, rich in the range and variety of emotional response. Several different temperaments are indicated, according to the other planetary conditions, but all of them are possible of great development.

The judicial capacity is highly developed, but there is no ability to carry out the plans so ably formulated. These people can think very clearly, with calm open minds that never lose sight of the objective, but they are not equipped to order an active, progressive existence, particularly in the modern business world.

The artistic talents of this group are in the field of designing, architecture, interior decorating, the fashion field and the theatre, mainly scenic and costume design, classical dancing, dramatics and theatrical direction.

Those born with this figure in the birth chart sometimes lean toward the mental degrees, and then the lifework is in the direction of law, university instruction, governmental diplomacy, higher mathematics, or if in commerce, the luxury trades.

The moon in this position is lavish in gifts, but the fundamental strength of which dependable characters are made is lacking. The natives of this position are more often than not morally weak. There is little backbone in this group, and they can never say no to themselves. In a way it is just as hard for them to say yes. It is seemingly impossible for them to make decisions, as both sides of a question always appear to have so much merit.

Therefore it can be seen that the moon in this position gives the artistic temperament, creative ability, a high type of mental understanding, but no executive ability, and little strength of character. The person is undependable and somewhat treacherous. Emotionally they are apt to be a puzzle. They look refined, chaste in habits and exceedingly selective. Actually they are voluptuous, deceptive in habits, with a voracious physical appetite.

For women this position allows more latitude. If they are engaged in the arts, the temperament is considered a rightful part of their make-up, and their success or failure is based upon the amount of application and stamina used to aid them in their work. They are not domestic in the accepted sense of the word, but they naturally adore love and marriage. Usually these women are so pretty and have so much charm that marriage is a foregone conclusion. However, the instability and weaknesses of the figure sometimes order a fatalistic ending to even this ambition.

For men the moon in Libra has many temperamental drawbacks to success. It makes them too changeable, too soft and too indeterminate. They are not sufficiently masculine or ruthless to insure success, and even when their lifework is suitable, and they are succeeding financially, their romantic experiences are often immoral and sometimes perverted. As with all lunations, there are plenty of natives leading well-ordered, normal lives, but the percentage of irregularity is found with the moon in Libra.

With both sexes the tendency toward erotic experience and perverted adventure is so strong that the native is caught in events and practices so extreme that the end is tragic. It is not unusual for these people to be caught in a tide of events that leads directly to untimely death.

When the rest of the chart is well balanced, the moon in Libra usually denotes great success in all partnerships. The seventh house is the house of partnerships, and with generally good planetary aspects the native is just, balanced, self-controlled and discerning. Here will be found all of the qualities necessary for the success of any partnership.

In the marriage relationship, this figure can denote a smoothly ordered existence, well balanced and well bred. The trend is toward the traditional in solidarity and permanence. Infidelity, which sometimes exists even in the best Libra household, is carried on with great secrecy and circumspection. A man with this figure in the chart attracts women of great distinction, usually women who all through the life exert influence over their husbands.

In the financial field, for all of the indecision and temperamental vagaries, these people with the moon in Libra make money. They frequently engage in highly paid professions, and when they are dependents it is usually where money is plentiful. The planetary scheme gives a nature so demanding of luxury and self-indulgence that the native would seek to fulfill this craving with every effort that their small capacity for application allows.

The physical make-up of natives in this birth scheme is not robust, but it is finely adjusted and healthy. Where the native is temperate, and in the average matters of health they are very much so, the system is seldom thrown out of balance. Illness is not usual among this group, and when they do fall ill the recuperative powers are very active.

When the moon is afflicted by the major planets, the result can be kidney trouble, ovarian weakness in women, Bright's disease, lumbago, diabetes, and bowel inflammation.

One of the most serious conditions faced by the people with the moon posited in Libra is mental derangement brought on by inward feelings so strong that the subject can no longer exercise control. Great grief, melancholy, jealousy, disappointment, or any of the major passions, allowed to take root with silent power, can upset this type of mentality and cause serious mental disorders.

THE MOON IN SCORPIO

People born with the moon in Scorpio have great strength of character, but they are handicapped by the tremendous weaknesses of the birth figure.

This position brings exaggerated sexual inclinations. These impulses spring from the very roots of the being and are so vicious and so strong that the native is their victim from the earliest youth throughout the life. The tendency here is a constant seeking after a new sensation, an unquenchable urge toward more indulgence and greater variety of experience. This inclination is accompanied by other indulgences, too much drinking and the ceaseless drive of emotional debauch.

With such a configuration it is easy to understand that all through the life dangers of one kind or another would threaten the health and the career. Oddly enough, these people have strength and dependability. They are often talented and pursue their work in the life with the same intensity that they bring to their vices. For this figure makes people of no small talents, and the proportions of everything that they do reaches out into the realms of the spirit.

Part of this lunation is a deep seeking after the occult.

The physical dimensions of this world are insufficient answers to all of the questions that the moon posited in Scorpio asks of life. These natives, when approaching middle age, delve into the secret places of the soul for the answer to the riddle of life. During the youth the eternal curiosity is there, but the chase for sexual experience and the lust for life push occult experimentation into the background. When the sexual fires have been somewhat slaked, other passions come into their own.

The excesses of this position are fully comprehended and the degrading quality well understood by the native, who is driven beyond himself by his desires, which are too strong for him to do other than satisfy. Long periods of self-abnegation and penance follow these debauches, for the subject is fully aware of just how low he has fallen.

The reproduction of the species is naturally part of the Scorpio rule, and since the make-up of people in this astrological scheme is a determined survival, this sexual curiosity is a part of their very soul.

For the men with this lunation in the birth scheme, there is usually a solution. If some degree of self-control is forced upon the native, if only for appearances before the outside world, his business or professional career can continue with a degree of dignity and success. A good deal of determination goes with this position, and therefore despite the unpleasant characteristics already mentioned, the native has resourcefulness and a sense of responsibility not so much to any individual or any group, but to himself. He is always determined to survive, and he owes it to himself to come out on top.

For the average women with the moon posited in Scorpio the situation is somewhat different. Even in the world of today she does not enjoy the freedom necessary to indulge her appetites safely; that is, not without danger in many departments of the life. Her vagaries often make her declassée, and her health is affected both through the body and the mind. Married women with this configuration have just as bad a time as single women. In the case of the married woman, her frenzied desires are never satisfied within her home. She is constantly seeking outside satisfaction. It is not hard to imagine the complications likely to result from such a scheme, and there are few women with this configuration who have not a good deal of scandal running through the life.

Professionally there is a good deal of success for both sexes in the right occupations. People born with this figure make good doctors and surgeons, chemists, research scientists, and dentists. They often choose embalming or any science connected with death. On the more spiritual plane, they may become teachers of occult philosophy, religion, and divinity; in the governmental field, secret service, criminal investigation, and trial law.

With the moon in Scorpio in the birth figure, the health is likely to suffer from outbursts of angry passion, and the possible losses and defeats of the past. Brooding and mental depression have the power to lower the vitality of these people, and their whole physical organism sometimes falls a prey to the violence of their emotions. If it were possible to foretell good health for any type of person through the wise use of the emotions and the temperate distribution of the life forces, this would be the kind of person who would enjoy a long, healthy, useful life.

Because of sexual abuses so general with this position, venereal diseases are the constant result. An afflicted moon brings the possibility of infections, rectal troubles, and internal colds causing various kinds of inflammation. Constipation and infection from lack of cleanliness are other dangers.

Women with an afflicted moon in Scorpio have health problems during their climacteric. During this period the dangers are blood disturbances, heart conditions, tumors of all types, circulatory diseases, and gallstones.

It must be remembered that this sign position brings an exaggerated taste for alcoholic liquors and the leaning toward drugs. This can be, if allowed to prevail, an evil of first magnitude. Since the planetary figure is surrounded by evils sufficiently serious, those that can be mastered by will power should be controlled at all costs.

THE MOON IN SAGITTARIUS

The moon in Sagittarius is the most intellectual luna position in the Zodiac. People with this birth figure will find themselves seeking knowledge wherever it is to be gleaned in the life. If they are the type that has found formal education beyond their financial reach, the natural impulse will be to study people and situations, and the instinctive reactions to the major problems of living will be superior to the average person's analysis of the same situations.

People born under a Sagittarian moon will be avid for the experiences of life, and spare themselves nothing when it comes to life's complications. They seek intrigue, and the more difficult and daring the outline of their lives, they better they like it.

These are very strong characters, with force, will power and the ability to execute their plans, no matter how daring. Luna Sagittarians have the greatest confidence in their own ability, and never for one moment doubt that anything they may conceive could be impractical or impossible. Frequently it is just that, for the daring of their conceptions does not always take into consideration that most of life's work is done along simple routine lines. However, what would be outrageous in people of other types is often quite successful when engineered by the Sagittarian type of thought. They are natural-born adventurers and gamblers, and even when of the highest type their philosophy is of the most remote and advanced school.

They are irked by anything small, and the proportions of their interests are all large, whether in business or that other field of speculative thought that is so much a part of their existence.

They are very infectious people, and their schemes sound perfectly wonderful. They have an interesting fluent flow of speech, and no other group, with the possible exception of the luna Gemini, talks any more or any better.

They talk so well that others are always the listeners, the learners and the buyers. They have a fine dramatic delivery, and even the simplest statements acquire importance when they deliver them. The one trouble here is that this ready speech can become gross exaggeration and very dangerous gossip.

Luna Sagittarians are not always so benevolent, but they are very humorous, and when they ridicule anyone, it is always to entertain a crowd at the victim's expense.

This birth figure produces wonderful actors. They are graceful and delightful to watch. They fill every gesture with meaning and effect. Their speech and rendition of lines is alive with charm. No other type can play a part to better advantage.

Sagittarius as a sign has always been regarded as the sportsman's sign. Luna Sagittarians are not so much inclined to violent hazardous outdoor sport. They are great walkers, and they do go in for outdoor life, but the stress here is to be placed on the active quality of the emotions and the mind.

Mentally Luna Sagittarians are voracious. They have a tremendous capacity for information, and they can absorb all sorts of subjects. Their interests are legion, and they attack each subject with equal vigor. Some of this activity is rather superficial. Not the interest—that is very sincere—but the digestion of the subject matter, when there are so many interests, must needs be rather incomplete. This same quality is true of the Gemini moon and seems to be a luna difficulty. When the moon gives an intellectual direction to the quality of thought, the digestion is apt to be so intuitive and rapid that popular belief describes it as too shallow to be thorough. This may or may not be true.

The mental qualities of the luna Sagittarian, while very wide, are considered somewhat impersonal. These people are interested in the progress of the world and anything that tends toward human betterment; mind over matter and the exaltation of the mental development of mankind interest them keenly. Individuals, in a personal sense, are less sacred to them. They may be capable of petty meannesses to individuals, but they are never disloyal to the interests of humanity.

The men of this birth figure are usually very successful. They are well equipped to succeed in the modern business world, and do not have to grub for the things that they desire. They are great spenders, and enjoy a jolly, pagan sort of social life, uninhibited and full of romantic interest. They are incurable woman-chasers and have put a great deal of enthusiasm into their dashing love affairs. As husbands, this love for variety is a little disconcerting to the wife. They do, however, select a very high type of woman, passionate, beautiful, and desirable.

Women having the moon posited in Sagittarius at birth are not quite as fortunate as the men. These women are highly intellectual, and frequently give their lives to "causes." They are handsome, serious-looking women, dignified and admirable, but they are not domestic; while they seek love and marriage, they do not seem to understand the use of those instinctive weapons that bring out marriage in the male quality of thought. They are in every way qualified to make the best of wives, and very often a man would get much more out of life married to the woman with this mental make-up than he does from mating with a possessive little female whose instinct is urging her to capture a protector.

People with the moon posited in Sagittarius have very

delicate nervous system's and a decided tendency to over-work themselves. They are very well balanced, on the plane of health, and all of their vital organs are well adjusted to a rapid pace. But they never stop to think of themselves, and drive their own bodies to collapse. Sometimes this nervous pressure externalizes itself in stuttering or some other defect of speech.

Accidents are frequent with this sign, and usually happen to the legs, hips and thighs. With an afflicted moon, there is a possibility of sciatica, rheumatism, nervous prostration, and hip disease. Many of the ills of this birth figure are not caused by organic disturbances, but are the result of accidents created by the recklessness of too much speed and too little judgment.

THE MOON IN CAPRICORN

The sign of Capricorn is not a sympathetic abode for the delicate, variable, sensitive, imaginative nature of the moon. But, moving in her chartered course in and out of the signs, she comes to rest, as she must in Capricorn.

Capricorn is cold, solitary, remote, repressed and obsessed. The people with this figure in the birth chart usually have a guiding thought, a mental mission, or an obsession, that often takes them their entire life to accomplish, whether for good or evil. If the other planets in the birth figure happen to be strongly favored by benign aspects, this "complex" may turn out to be a beneficial influence. But, even if this were not the case, the mental make-up of the Capricorn lunation would force some manifestation of the native's determined obsession.

The entire temperament bestowed by this luna vibration is grim, repellent and solitary. The native has intelligence, force, strength, both of mind and body, but the qualities that go to make up a social human being, happily adjusted to the life, are completely absent. The native is selfish and covetous, a prey to the inward passions that we have all been taught to erase from our consciousness. They criticize others without mercy, but envy them the very qualities that they revile. With this aspect the luna vibrations for evil are much stronger than the solar forces of the same quality.

People having this type of lunation are very strong-minded, so that it is never weakness that fosters their evil spirit, but lively malific, self-seeking ambitions, backed by a keen brain always on the lookout for victory at someone else's expense.

It is the strength of this position that makes it so dangerous. If a weak man chooses to do wrong, he may be caught in the act, or his plans may fail for lack of power. Any number of things may happen to the project before it is fulfilled, but when a strong, clever person decides to do evil, his plot has the benefit of robust construction. Down through history many of the world's famous tyrants as well as reformers had this lunation of the moon posited in Capricorn. There is in the make-up of all these people, however much they may have differed in purpose, a similar point of view and quality of thought. This is somewhat fanatical, and always so introspective that the subject is bound up in his own conception of right. Those of the group not concerned with a moral value, but concentrating on personal gain, will be just as blind to the errors involved by this point of view. It is not unusual for this type of complete personal concentration to evolve a genius.

This position is quite good for men in a worldly sense. A man with this configuration is usually impersonal in his judgment of the world around him, but he is very selfish regarding his own aims and ambitions. He is cautious, thrifty, and lays his plans systematically. He seldom makes intimate friends, and usually confides in nobody. His interests are in the commercial world, and his greatest successes are usually in business. Government and politics offer other fertile fields for the type of ability found in this personality.

Despite the temperamental coldness of the type, these men

usually marry. They do not seek romantic love, but rather a partnership based on mutual cooperation. They are very reliable, and take responsibility seriously. If for any reason they become interested in women outside of the home environment, this attitude will become one of permanent infidelity. Usually they are great defenders of their own actions, as this is a type that always likes to be right. In one way or another they manage to make themselves appear to be the injured party. In fact, there is always an urge toward evil in every gesture of this personality.

The women with this position in the native chart are somewhat different. As individuals they are less perverse, and much less sinister in thought. They are austere, masculine in temperament, and intellectual. Life it not very friendly to this type of woman, and all of her ambitions and longings are apt to meet with delays, obstacles and frustration. Most of her difficulties come through a lack of domesticity in the innate disposition, and a desire to live her life in an atmosphere of masculine competition. They are very devoted women, who can be trusted with deep secrets, great works, and responsibilities of any kind. They have high standards, and live up to an exalted code of right and wrong. It seems too bad that the types of women so well suited to be the companions of the best varieties of men are often scratched from the list of competitors by the most superficial qualities in the nature of women. If these women were more light-minded, sensitive and whimsical, their matrimonial chances would be increased.

The health of this group is excellent. They are strong, sturdy people with excellent constitutions. They can work long and hard before any effects are seen on the cast-iron of their endurance. They worry a great deal and sometimes this has a more disastrous effect on their health than long hours and intense concentration. The general tendency of the position is to brood inwardly over real or fancied wrongs. This condition is dangerous and has been known to destroy the entire digestion. A wholesome diet is very important, and the heavy foods, sharp seasonings and indigestible combinations liked by people of this kind are harmful to them.

As life goes on there is an increasing tendency toward rheumatism, colitis, and all kinds of indigestion. Skin affections and teeth troubles are part of the weaknesses of this position.

THE MOON IN AQUARIUS

The position of the moon in this sign is one of the best of the twelve. It is described in this superlative way for the following reasons:

The moon, naturally variable in influence, has considerable stability in this sign. The lack of heart and frigidity apparent in several of the other luna figures is quite absent in the lunation from Aquarius. The force dispensed from this urge is warm, humane and stimulating.

People with this lunation in the natal chart are apt to be very intelligent, evenly-balanced people with a happy, optimistic quality of thought. They are full of ideas, and have more ability to put their thoughts into active practice than people of any of the other intellectual positions of this sort (with the possible exception of the moon in Sagittarius).

These people are tolerant, perceptive, humane in their impulses toward mankind, and always willing to give more than they get. They have no petty selfishness and no small jealousies. They give themselves whole-heartedly to any service that they undertake, and they are usually not only capable but inventive. A plan of action or scheme of endeavor under the management of this type of person frequently benefits from their practical improvements.

The high types of this group make wonderfully rounded persons. They have, in addition to the more universal virtues already mentioned, pleasant, kindly dispositions in private or domestic life. The less exalted type of luna Aquarian is good-natured and easy-going, but lacks the ability and strength of purpose found in the noble type.

The negative variety of luna Aquarian is sometimes very eccentric, and encourages great unconventionality in the domestic life. For the rest, the existence is purposeless, and all of the noble accomplishment so current in the life of Aquarians is dissipated in idle activities with "arty" groups.

Aquarians in the highest meaning of the term are public characters. Professional men, scholars, teachers, ministers, and specialists in any department serving humanity. They are tolerant, diplomatic, helpful to others in their own field, and ideal workers at whatever holds their intellectual interests. Sometimes this position produces a genius, but such a condition requires rather more personal "wire-pulling" than the moon in Aquarius signifies. By this is meant that the native will give of himself to his cause so unstintingly that if self-aggrandizement is to be gained, it must come as a result of outside recognition rather than as the outcome of any stimulation brought on by the native.

This temperament, considered apart from its special character of social servitor, is highly individual. Many eccentricities and peculiarities are a part of these people's make-up. They are rather unconventional, and live their own lives quite unaffected by comment or criticism. They have a gift for making friends, and are often helped by influential people, exactly as they themselves are ready to help others. There is nothing personal or possessive in the attitude of these people, and they can endure loneliness, privation and periods of waiting better than other more acquisitive types.

The faults most common among this group are procrastination, vain promises, and the inability to force any circumstance that takes a measure of destruction to a conclusion.

The men of this group when engaged in scholarly pursuits and work that brings out their ability, succeed very well in the world. They are seldom discouraged by struggle, and the development of their work is often just as important to them as fulfilment. They seldom have a smooth domestic life, for their inclinations are unconventional, and they seem to draw to them complic ted situations that take a lifetime to simplify.

The women that they choose are high-bred and cultured, but there is frequently a cloud hanging over the domestic atmosphere. Either there are separations to be bridged or marriage tangles to be unraveled. When the situation is finally cleared of complications, this type of man makes an ideal companion in the life.

Lunar Aquarian women are rather masculine in their outlook on life. They love the business and professional world, where they are so capable and so successful. When they do marry, they make the best of parents, as they have plenty of patience, kindness, intelligence and understanding. They are so unselfish that the child is naturally their first consideration. But, since the temperament of so many women with the Aquarian lunation in the birth figure is completely masculine in appearance, they enjoy less opportunity to be parents than other types that are not nearly so well equipped.

Unfortunately, this is the type of woman who not only has a masculine kind of mind, but an unfeminine appearance as well. She has no sex appeal and feels in no way constrained to simulate anything of the kind. There is no attempt to soften the exterior, and the mind lacks tenderness as well as artifice.

In matters of health these natives must beware of nervous prostration. Another avenue through which disease may attack is the lungs. An afflicted moon could bring about anaemia, blood poisoning, and one or another of the social diseases. In extreme cases some of the mental disorders have resulted. A certain amount of rest and relaxation is a necessity with this type of person.

THE MOON IN PISCES

This figure in the birth chart creates a great many problems in the life for its natives.

The position is highly occult, and fills the spirit with vain, indefinable longings. The spirit reaches out toward realms unknown, and the whole intelligence is withdrawn from the physical of this world, or even the higher planes of the intellect. The person scarcely knows what he or she really seeks. Nothing in this life measures up to their dreams, and possessions have no value. They are weary of the struggle for existence, and any aspiration, no matter how impossible of attainment gives them the chance to stretch the wings of the spirit.

On the other hand, life in this world has its own insistence, and the will to live struggles with the luna Piscean's desire for death.

The average person with this configuration in the natal scheme does not experience anything so definite in the way of a call from the beyond. Rather, natives become bored with the regular routine of life, and seek sensational outlets for their depressed nerves, and enervated spirit. For the character that is not strong, this is dangerous. Eager, simple minds have too often through uncontrolled morbid curiosity sought solace and stimulation for the spirit, and ended up a slave to the drug habit, or to the spiritualistic mediums.

Even for the average daily routine, this planetary influence is not helpful. The natives are uncertain in all the gestures of life. Indecision is the keynote of the character. They are diffident, negative and vacillating, and stubbornly work against any practical judgments they are forced to make by the natural duties of life. Everything must, in order to please them, have a touch of the ideal. They are usually disappointed with the outcome of anything they tackle, for the end could never measure up to their ideals. It never occurs to them that part of their disappointment is founded on their inability to accomplish any task simply or correctly. This type of person chooses the hard way to do everything, and gets little systematic practice in any field of work. They do not apply themselves consistently, even though they are patient and docile in disposition.

Naturally this temperament unrestricted runs natives into a great deal of unhappiness. They become melancholy, brooding and oversensitive, and while they sit viewing life as they would like it to be, the procession marches on without them.

Natives in this group are very talented. They are artistic, and love and understand beauty. They are creative, responsive and intuitive, and have a soulful poetic type of ability when expressing themselves in the artistic fields. They can succeed as writers, musicians, poets, artists and designers. They fit in very well in the theatrical business, in fact in all branches of the arts, provided they can stimulate enough energy and fixity of purpose to succeed.

The personal lives of people born with this figure in the birth chart are apt to have a large proportion of self-sacrifice, loneliness and renunciation in the life's experience. Pisces is the sign of tears, sorrow and isolation. This fact, coupled with the natives' natural desire for "sainthood" or martyrdom often works toward a demonstration of just this condition in the life. Sometimes these people turn to work in the prisons, and use their highly-developed intuitive faculties for the purpose of criminal investigation. Sometimes they use their deep human sympathies for criminal and prison reform.

Many luna Pisceans with strength of character bestowed by other planetary forces in the birth chart give boundless charity in many fields. There is no other sign so sympathetic with human ills and human suffering. When the character has some direction these people rise to great heights of service to humanity and produce a divine combination of spiritual purity and good work in the world.

Weak luna Pisceans, coming under the domination of Neptune's negative forces, are deceitful, lying, incompetent, lazy, and a prey to any self-indulgent force or vice that happens to take possession of the mind.

Men having this figure in the birth scheme have much to fight. It is expected of a man that he face the realities of this world with singleness of purpose and strength of mind. The position brings with it a good deal of indecision and spiritual discontent, and even when the commercial life harmonizes with the whole scheme, the restless implications are there. The seeker after solace is sure to find trouble in one form or another. Excesses and various abuses are the frequent outcome of this position, unless the native is strong minded and sublimates his urges in intellectual occupation or artistic work.

For women the position is not so difficult. More latitude is allowed a woman for her temperamental discontent, and she can often find satisfaction and relief in religion, art, and service to some charity. When she takes the more mysterious and dangerous road along some of the occult sciences, she frequently ends up the victim of wicked fraud, or a nervous wreck.

Domestically both sexes are enthusiastic and satisfied with home life. They are personal, possessive people, very affectionate and cooperative in the home. They are easily influenced by the other partner, and give plenty of love and affection to the marriage relationship. As a class they adore beauty, and if the husband is a luna Piscean, he is most likely to select a beautiful wife whose every word will be a law to him, and whom he will indulge and adore for the balance of his life.

Women with this position in the birth figure make devoted wives. They are unstinting in their will to give, sympathetic and harmonious, and put a great deal of inspiration into the marriage relationship.

The physical make-up of these people is not robust. They

are susceptible to contagious diseases, and have very little resistance against colds, chills, sore throats, etc. An afflicted moon gives a leaning toward lung trouble, pneumonia, melancholia and complaints of the feet. Sometimes this sign, when under bad planetary aspects, brings a possibility of the social diseases.

Love, Romance
& Marriage

ASTROLOGICAL LOVE NATURE

Certain Zodiacal types are naturally drawn to each other. Every birth figure has a certain kind of Venus, Mars, Jupiter, Uranus, Neptune and Moon. In its way, each one of these planets plays a big part in the love nature and in the possible success of the love life.

The average person thinks only of Venus in connection with love, but several of the other planets play equally serious parts in the romantic ventures of life. Jupiter and Uranus control a much deeper side of the love life than either Venus or Mars. The Moon has a decided effect on every person's romantic fate. A brief outline of what the planets mean to the lover will give each person an idea of what to expect of the love life, and what to look for in choosing a sweetheart or a husband.

141

Venus in the particular house and sign of your horoscope controls the material nature of love, the kind of love you are capable of, the place where you might seek it, and the weapons used to ensnare it.

The character and position of Mars in the birth chart have, among other functions in the life, the power to intensify the physical love. Mars can make the sex urges more violent, potent, and sometimes less pure.

While Jupiter has many other far-reaching influences in the average chart, there are positions where he can greatly enhance romantic opportunities. In a woman's horoscope the moon in friendly relationship to Jupiter can indicate a very advantageous marriage.

Uranus, when occupying the same degree and sign position of the sweetheart's moon in the birth chart, indicates a deep, powerful magnetism between the two natures, a force far stronger and more lasting than the urge of Venus.

The position and quality of Neptune in the birth chart give sentiment and sentimentality to the affectional nature. Many of the other qualities that make for attractive emotional appeal are made by the blend of Neptune and Venus or Neptune and the Moon.

Therefore it is easy to see how persons might meet, become attracted to each other on the crest of some astrological wave and finally marry, to suffer later during the long years from basic unbalance in the natures, and fundamental friction.

The first step toward the choice of a mate is through the sun sign. The fire signs are all harmonious to each other, and the same rule applies to the air, earth and water signs. That means that Aries, Leo and Sagittarius people all get along very well together. The dates of these birthdays are as follows:

Aries, from March 21 to April 19.

Leo, July 23 to August 23.

Sagittarius, November 23 to December 21.

These groups make sympathetic companions to each other. They have somewhat the same basic natures in that they are all three generous, warm, passionate, sincere, dominant and idealistic.

This does not mean that only people born in the same elemental group can possibly live together in harmony. In fact, the fire signs give each other a little too much generosity and no play for give and take. Several of the other elements blend very well, and the harmonious combinations for the fire signs are as follows:

Aries people are well aspected to Gemini and Aquarius of the air trinity. The mental quickness of these airy personalities appeal to fiery, energetic Aries.

Aries birthdays come from March 21 to April 19.

Gemini birthdays come from May 21 to June 21.

Aquarius birthdays come from January 20 to February 18.

Leo people get a fine response from Libra and Gemini. The innate taste, high-bred appearance, and natural good breeding of the Libra person, often satisfies the Leo craving for a mate who is a credit to the home.

Leo birthdays come from July 23 to August 23.

Libra birthdays come from September 24 to October 23.

Gemini birthdays come from May 21 to June 21.

The Sagittarian personality could find great companionship with either Aquarius or Libra. The Aquarian intellect, plus the eternal desire to serve mankind is very sympathetic to Sagittarian interests, and the unconventional Aquarian would greatly enjoy the dramatic, humorous, vital Sagittarian.

Sagittarian birthdays come from November 23 to December 21.

Aquarian birthdays come from January 20 to February 18.

Libra birthdays come from September 24 to October 23.

People born in the air trinity make harmonious marriage partners for each other, even though there is a thought too much coolness and impersonality in the make-up of all three types. It makes for a rather too formal marriage if both partners can politely dispense with the company of the other. However, the fundamental intelligence harmonizes, so that much can be built upon that hope.

Aquarius birthdays come from January 20 to February 18.

Libra birthdays come from September 24 to October 23.

Gemini birthdays come from May 21 to June 21.

It has already been shown how well the air signs harmonize with the fire signs and what particular divisions of each class create good companions for each other.

The earth trinity harmonizes, these signs being Taurus, Virgo and Capricorn. These divisions, but especially Virgo and Capricorn, do not mate well with other signs of the Zodiac. In the case of the Virgo native, almost the only type that is wholly suitable for their temperament are other people born in the same sign. These birthdays are as follows:

Taurus, from April 20 to May 20.

Capricorn, from December 22 to January 19.

Virgo, from August 24 to September 23.

Taurus people do blend quite well with Cancer and Pisces, more especially when the Taurus type is a man married to either a Cancer or Pisces wife. All three groups are great home lovers, affectionate and agreeable.

The weakness of the two latter types are feminine in character, and would not injure the home life of the family; that is, if all other conditions in the birth charts were reasonably good.

Pisces birthdays are from February 19 to March 20.

Cancer birthdays are from June 22 to July 22.

Taurus birthdays are from April 20 to May 20.

Sometimes Capricorn marries happily with Pisces. This combination had best be a Pisces woman with a Capricorn man. There is great strength in the Capricorn type and a Pisces woman is usually very clinging and dependent. They are also somewhat self-indulgent, and the stern, uncompromising Capricorn nature would bring out the idealism and spirituality of Pisces, and curb the laxity as well. On the other hand, the warmth and devotion of the Pisces love nature would infuse happiness into the life of a Capricornian. It is very hard for Capricorn types to be happy, and it takes a great deal of emotional encouragement to make them trusting and contented.

Scorpio men sometimes make good husbands for Capricorn women. The Scorpio man is very jealous and exacting, and the austere virtues of the Capricorn woman, coupled with her sound mind and many capabilities, might satisfy even his exactions that she be both trustworthy and clever.

The Scorpio birthdays are from October 24 to November 22.

The Pisces birthdays are from February 19 to March 20.

The Capricorn birthdays are from December 22 to January 19.

The water trinity are considered harmonious to each other. These signs are Pisces, Scorpio and Cancer, and the birthdays are as folllows:

Pisces, from February 19 to March 20.

Scorpio, from October 24 to November 22.

Cancer, from June 22 to July 22.

Most of the other signs harmonizing well with the water trinity have already been mentioned. The possible exception is a Cancer mating with Virgo. This is favorable provided the Cancer native is a woman, and the husband is born in Virgo. Loving, whimsical, domestic Cancer, could put great trust in competent Virgo. The emotional response from Virgo is adequate from the viewpoint of affections, but sorely lacking in vital, primitive passions. The birthday of Cancer is from June 22 to July 22, and the birthday of Virgo is from August 24 to September 23.

In order to test out the love nature of a man or a woman and discover just the right emotional type for marriage, it is advisable to know in what sign Venus was posited at birth.

VENUS IN ARIES

Venus is very weak in Aries. The activity of the sign is too ruthless, and the pace of energy too fast for the light, material character of Venus. The planet is not enhanced by the dashing Aries idealism, and the domestic leanings of Venus are not encouraged by Aries. Aries is a sign of accomplishment in the outer world, and the Venus thought of personal development is not helped by Aries. Aries makes the love nature fiery, impetuous, demanding, but also giving. It makes it a generous ardent fleeting set of impulses. An Aries Venus is masculine in thought, a real young Lochinvar lover who rides gallantly in, but also rides away.

VENUS IN TAURUS

Venus is very powerful in Taurus. It is the ruler of the sign, and people with Venus in Taurus may expect to find a material atmosphere around their love life. They will seek wealthy mates, and even if the planet is opposed by other forces, the chances are that their persistence and patient pursuit will finally win the love and position they are seeking. The fortunes of the person with Venus in this position are apt to vary, but here is a determined urge toward domestic contentment, worldly love, and the satisfaction of the personal ambitions. This is a rather ruthless Venus, tireless in her quest for love and the material good things of life. The love nature here is deep, secret and unchanging, with feminine intensity and masculine strength. The person is apt to have a great sexual appetite and be very satisfying in the responses to love.

VENUS IN GEMINI

Venus is moderately strong in Gemini. She has a very material outlook in this sign, and when found in this position in the horoscope of a woman, the tendencies will be for gold digging. The emotional life or any romantic goal when controlled by Venus in this sign is often attained through trickery, triumph over rivals, and all of the camouflage possible under the circumstances. The love nature itself is youthful, airy, mercurial, and full of sunshine and clouds. The touch of the lover is exceedingly light, bantering, flirtatious and fleeting.

VENUS IN CANCER

Venus has a very maternal quality in Cancer. Those with Venus in this sign at birth will seek love through their ability to mother and protect. The instincts of this Venus are softly melancholy and brooding. Here is an urge to tend the home, bring up a family, and nourish every member of the household. These natives must love, possess and serve something, and their natural outlet is home and family. When, as sometimes happens, larger issues enter the life, the object of affection is merely service to humanity or to God. In most cases Venus fulfills the personal urge of this sign, be it man or woman, (although this is a feminine Venus) and she fills the native with power to draw love through devotion to the home ideals. This love is very deep and passionate, protective and nourishing.

VENUS IN LEO

The sign of Leo is a very vital sign, so that any planet found posited there at Birth will have a good deal of energy. Therefore a Leo-Venus is vital, hot, passionate, almost overpoweringly generous and inspiring, but not fruitful. The nature of Leo is arid, like the sun, and planets coming under this dominion reflect something of its character. People having Venus posited in Leo achieve their romantic ambitions through their own efforts and the force of their personality. They have plenty of energy to pursue their desires and are rich in the magnetism to attract. The standards of Leo are so high and the romantic conceptions so lofty that few measure up to the ideals of the Leo-Venus. The

results are often people with the love life tragically unful-
filled.

Venus in Virgo

Venus is weak in Virgo. The natures of the sign and the
planet do not harmonize. It goes deeper than this. The basic
qualities of Virgo are not food for Venus, therefore this
emotional urge is starved and stunted. People with Venus
posited in this sign usually attain their romantic ends, such
as they are, through flattery, courting the beloved, and a
painstaking personal service. The lover is apt to be persistent. The first to come and last to leave, in fact, he wears
his adversary out. Usually his ambitions lead him to the
beloved, and he courts some sort of material betterment
through love.

In a woman's natal figure this type of Venus frequently
gives her a chaste, fragile look (when she is very young)
that has great appeal for the more spiritually minded man,
or the man who is very jealous. This chaste appearance wears
off later in life, and freezes into cool, impersonality that is
mighty disappointing when translated into the emotional
nature. This kind of woman has no power to give herself,
and her whole ideology of romantic love is distorted.

Venus in Libra

Venus is at the peak of her power in Libra, where she
may be considered in her own highest octave. She is the
ruler of this sign, and people who have her posited in Libra
at birth make the most interesting romancers of all types.
They should always use a beautiful, high-minded, esthetic
approach to love. Their actions should be well-bred and
their whole behavior as a lover or sweetheart should be one
of gracious appreciation. This sign influence is very delicately proportioned between the male and the female; therefore, with Venus posited in the sign at birth, the balance of
the sexes might easily be disturbed. Homosexuals and some-

times prostitutes are found with Venus in Libra. These people are among the most passionate of all types, and their sense of the exquisite leads them to glorify perversion, and perform the erotic in sex like a ritual. Those who are more happily balanced make the most desirable if not the most permanent mates in the Zodiac.

Venus in Scorpio

Venus is at her very weakest in Scorpio. Her influence here is sensual and profligate at best, and her strength no equal ballast for the dark passions of Scorpio. The native with this configuration in the birth figure is apt to pursue love with great extravagance of courtship. These people would exact and give a very demonstrative love, and be exceedingly physical in their practices.

They might seek to enslave the beloved by catering to some physical vice or at least some sensuality that would create an affair both intense, erotic and abnormal. In less exaggerated cases the lover is simply passionate with a tremendous appetite for sex. This is a jealous, demanding attitude. but it is also an extremely devoted and generous one.

Venus in Sagittarius

Venus is considered the lower octave of Jupiter, and Jupiter is the ruler of Sagittarius. Some of the gifts of Venus on the material plane are also a part of the Jupiter character; for instance, extravagance in thought and pocketbook, cheer, charm and good temper when well aspected. Therefore the relationship between this sign and Venus is friendly, although Venus is only moderately powerful in the sign. Actually the proportions of Sagittarius are too vast for the limited powers of Venus. The person with this aspect in the birth figure will seek love through the use of influence, power, and worldly favors. A woman with this aspect may have superior qualities and marry far above her station in life. She is likely to be very ambitious, jealous of her standing and reputation, and gifted in many ways. Men having this birth position will seek a social existence in some group that is distinguished in one way or another. They are likely to have a polished sophisticated manner, be well educated, and have all the outward trappings of success.

VENUS IN CAPRICORN

Venus is not at her best in this sign, and those with this birth figure are apt to have little warmth in the love nature. They approach their romantic ambitions timidly, without confidence, and an innate knowledge that they are romantically handicapped.

This is a very practical figure, and Venus here uses her charms to gain material benefits. This sign often indicates some measure of self-sacrifice, and with Venus in this birth sign, especially if afflicted, the chances are that love will be sacrificed to gain material benefit.

If we find Venus posited in Capricorn in a woman's chart, her appearance may be most romantic, tall and statuesque, with large somber, brooding eyes, but her temperament will be very practical. Her interests will be largely on the date of the marriage and whether the suitor can support her properly. She will take her duties as a wife seriously, and in a material way prove a fine wife. Emotionally she is apt to prove a bit austere, and somewhat of a checkrein on the husband who would make a rollicking game of love. For the man with Venus in this birth sign, he is apt to bury his secret romantic leanings if they do not fit in with his ambitions. He feels that to enjoy love is a little bit wrong anyway, and he cannot quite understand how other men remain good men and indulge their physical passions. From his point of view, a man falls when he accedes to love. If this type of man was lucky enough to have a wife who could disabuse him of these ideas, he would be a much happier man.

Venus in Aquarius

This position of Venus in the birth chart often makes what is described as "ladies and gentleman." These people have a well-bred, gracious manner, and they display intelligence and taste in the life. They use tact and diplomacy to secure the coveted loves and romances of existence, and they have so much in their favor that success is usually theirs for the asking. This position is not one of fiery passion, but rather a subtle exchange of the refinements of passion. A satisfaction of the desire for companionship, home building, joint career building, and intellectual harmony. Both men and women of this type are ideally attractive to other people, but they themselves are exceedingly fussy and discriminating in their choice of a mate; and buried under all of their highsounding selection is a streak of common sense that seeks dignity and decency in the loved one.

Venus in Pisces

Venus is exalted in Pisces and in one of her most powerful positions in the Zodiac. Here Venus is in her own element combined with a sign character that expands her lush sensuousness and all of her sympathetic virtues. This Neptunian Venus makes her natives approach their dream of love with a silent, spiritual, insinuating appeal that works slowly and secretly through the heart of the beloved until the capture is made. These are very devoted people, often serving the loved one with the most delightful attentions, never failing in the romantic appeal, regardless of which sex is doing the wooing. Women with this figure in the birth chart are better suited to the quality of the position than are the men. The softness of the temperament is naturally womanly and very fruitful. Women of this type are beautiful, and carry an indefinable aura of love in their appearance and manner. They seem to fill every act of love with a tender graciousness, and they raise the whole physical performance of sex up to the highest spiritual rapture. On the other hand, when Venus is afflicted it can somewhat change the picture. Either the ultimate goal of the native's desires must be attained over tremendous odds, or the love nature is perverted through muddled impulses of spirit and flesh.

Family &
Friendship

YOUR MATE ACCORDING TO BIRTHDAY

After the general rules offered for the best harmony between the types, and the additional romantic personality information added by the position of Venus in the signs, it will be helpful to read an analysis of the wives and husbands created by the sign-characters of the Zodiac. Just find the division of your wife's or husband's birthday, and read the suggestions for the better understanding of each other.

THE ARIES WIFE

March 21 to April 19

Some signs of the Zodiac, regardless of whether they are masculine or feminine signs, make better women than men, or vice-versa. Aries is a very masculine sign, but the Aries men are not often pure types, and then much of the strength of the sign is dissipated. The Aries women personalizes one of the highest womanly developments of the Zodiac.

These women make wonderful wives for ambitious men. They have brilliant independent minds and healthy bodies. They like to spend their spare time in some constructive self-improvement and are witty, clever conversationalists with wonderful social presence. Either they are willing to help the husband in business, or they have some lucrative side line of their own that adds to the family fortunes, for they are rather unconventional women and seek the unusual outlet. This type of wife is *never* found bolstered up on a day bed amidst piles of cushions, true-story periodicals, nerve sedatives, and half-empty coffee cups. She is efficient, wide-awake, generous and companionable.

Her appearance is very smart, for she is usually a good-looking woman who takes great pride in her appearance. Pride is also one of her outstanding qualities. She has such a superior opinion of her own family that it shows quite plainly in her behavior, and sometimes causes others to be jealous and resentful.

Jealousy and a desire for a competitive social life are two of her worst faults. She is apt to be jealous of her husband's attentions, and may have a vivid imagination where her wrongs are concerned. She knows that she is good, and wants her husband to concentrate upon her with great intensity and never praise any one else. This type of woman is happiest married to a passionate, possessive man, one who makes her own sense of possession seem fragile by comparison. She should not have a moment in which to seek grievances, and she is at her best showing the rarest side of her character, self-sacrifice for her family.

When family life rolls along smoothly, this type of wife is rather extravagant. She is so generous that she frequently overdoes the giving for family and friends, and often makes people uncomfortable by the weight of their obligation to her, which she is never quite willing that they repay.

As a wife, the Aries woman would be most happy married to an aggressively masculine man. Sometimes the dominant woman attracts a recessive sort of man. This is not good for the Aries woman, whose activity in the home and demonstration to her husband would soon appear to submerge the man of the family. For this type of woman such a condition might mean the death of love. She loves only the man she can greatly admire, and his ability to control her is an important part of her devotion to him. If his hold over her is dominant, especially an impetus toward development, and his constitution is very virile, she is his for life.

THE ARIES HUSBAND

March 21 to April 19

The Aries husband, when found somewhat near the pure type, is a very distinguished, desirable sort of man. He is the kind of looking man that all girls aspire to, but who is by appearance and temperament a little hard to acquire. This is because he is naturally exceedingly fussy, and rather like the Leo man, exacting in his ideals. He has a romantic mental picture of what he wants in a wife, and this mental picture demands perfection. The lady must be beautiful, clever, and very good.

These men are conventional in thought, and do not go in for bohemian types in romance. They demand a high moral code in the women of their choice, regardless of their own private irregularities, which may take the form of an isolated adventurous fling. As a matter of fact, the Aries man hates clandestine affairs. He is outspoken to a fault, and refuses to hide anything that he feels like doing. He considers it a personal affront that he should have to look outside of his home for love, but he is rather demanding sexually, and if he is not gratified, he will look elsewhere.

The Aries man is ardent, proud, full of personality, and all through the life makes a romantic appeal to the woman he marries. About the most difficult problem in the married life of the Aries man is to satisfy his romantic conceptions of physical love. He has a voracious appetite, which he will not sublimate. No substitute devotion satisfies him, but a wife can gain his everlasting faithfulness if she harmonizes with him physically.

THE TAURUS WIFE

April 20 to May 20

The Taurus wife is perhaps the most devoted and dependable kind of wife in the whole range of Zodiacal types. She never resorts to divorce and endures extreme hardship rather than desert her mate. Naturally when making this statement, the devotion of the Cancer wife, and the Leo wife rises up to contest the assertion. But, the Taurus wife has a nature peculiarly adapted to domestic life as we have designed it. She is the perfect home-maker. She is a devoted mother and a loving wife, satisfied with her husband's efforts in her behalf. These efforts are usually quite ambitious, for Taurus women are pushing in a secret way. They appear to be calm, reserved and everybody's friend, but underneath they are as jealous as the Aries woman, and covet the rich, worldly things of life. The Aries wife's jealousy is for her husband's devotion, but the Taurus wife's passions are covetous and material. Her husband's devotion is something that she never questions, largely because it seldom strays. She is a very affectionate, demonstrative woman, wholly engrossed in her home and family, which she watches with a personal attention that not only serves, but exacts service from them. Beneath the goodness of the Taurus wife there is a determined persistent streak that uses the husband to further in every way her desire to enjoy life. She makes herself very dependent, although she can really help herself if necessary.

The devotion of these women can best be held by a successful type of man, the kind of husband who is important in the business world and can afford to give his wife a luxurious home, where she may show off her really wonderful housekeeping ability and social charm.

THE TAURUS HUSBAND

April 20 to May 20

The Taurus husband has the finest qualities of all of the signs for a successful husband. There have been some descriptions of the Taurus man characterizing him as rather immoral. It is true that there is a bullish tendency to satisfy the intense physical urge so potent in this native. But the Taurus man makes so devoted a husband, so dependable, kind, generous and faithful to his trust as a home-builder that the violence of his emotional nature must be overlooked. He never neglects his home for any outside interest, which when it intrudes is very transitory and fleeting.

This type of husband adores his wife and children, and strains every effort to give them the best home, education, clothes and amusements that his world provides. These men often marry above their station in life, partly because they are so ambitious to establish themselves, and partly because their worldly success leads them toward higher social circles. The rulership of Venus in the sign gives them a great appreciation of beauty, and in order to hold a Taurus husband throughout the life the wife must look beautiful and behave lovingly. These husbands adore dependence, and always like to feel that they are the sole providers of their families' happiness. Domestic life, which palls from time to time on so many of the other Zodiacal types, is never tiresome to the Taurus husband. Once married, he never seeks the bachelor existence, or even thinks back regretfully over the liberty that he never counted as precious.

THE GEMINI WIFE

May 21 to June 21

This type of wife is first and foremost an intellectual woman. The strongest appeal is mental companionship and the ability to make her feel that she is a partner in living, rather than a housekeeper, or even a maternal guide. It is natural for a woman of this kind to keep up her outside activities after marriage, particularly if she has a talent worthy of development. Of course outside activities take up a lot of time, and many husbands resent this diffusion of interests. However, if there is to be harmony in the home it is somewhat better to treat this condition tactfully. Sometimes the wife herself discovers that two separate existences are impossible if justice is to be done, and she gradually gives up her business career. In many cases the Gemini woman is so capable that her home and her work are managed very smoothly. When these natives are talented it is usually in some well paid line, for they are not the long-suffering type that works for nothing. They have been called mercenary, as they rate themselves very highly, and demand just compensation for their efforts.

Gemini women are particular how their homes are run, even if they are not in them as much as other wives. They are very refined, meticulous women who abhor untidiness, and though they seldom do their own work, they direct efficiently and command obedience.

The Gemini woman shines brightly in society. She is scintillating, well informed and worldly, and is the kind of woman who would make a helpful wife for a professional man. A doctor, or a lawyer, who builds his practice on agreeable social contacts would find this type of woman the very partner for his interests.

This nativity gives a somewhat flirtatious nature, and many a husband watches this type of wife with anxiety. He would feel much better if he knew that she was just using her sharp wits to enjoy a battle of words. Her common sense and protective instinct are very strong, and she would never sacrifice her home and husband for what she of all people knows to be a little conversational romance.

THE GEMINI HUSBAND

May 21 to June 21

This is not the kind of husband for the possessive, passionate wife. These men are interesting persons, talented, intellectual, and social. Most often they are found working in the professions as draftsmen, newspaper men, writers, or scientists of many kinds. Their domestic life is sketchy. This type of man looks for a marriage partner who can share his mental interests, who is never tied to her home, and is willing to change her environment as often as her husband desires to vary the scenery. The wives of these men must learn to bear with the husband's general interest in people, or other women. He is inclined to be flirtatious, but his wandering fancy is never to be taken seriously. Actually Gemini men have a great deal of common sense, and while they love to pursue the will o' the wisp of variety, no other kind of man can close a romantic chapter with more finality, especially when he knows that he has something to lose by a flirtation. If the Gemini husband could find a wife who gave direction to his life, and personalized his interest in wife and family without nagging him or stressing this fact too much, many of these natives would be more successful.

THE CANCER WIFE

June 22 to July 22

The Cancer wife mothers everything. She typifies the most motherly influence of all of the Zodiacal wives. When at her best, she is a sympathetic, affectionate protective woman, patient, devoted, adaptable, satisfied with anything her husband provides for her. Her home is wherever her husband decides that it should be, and she gives the humblest place a permanent, established look. Her presence is sanctifying, and she understands how to serve. She is loved and respected in return for her devotion, and is the personification of all of the literature written that idealizes "Mother."

All this, of course, depends upon the planetary combinations in the nativity. Many Cancer wives have some of these good qualities. They are devoted mothers, full of affection for the family, but too often moody, changeable, ignorant, and unwilling to be improved, temperamental to a fault and sensitive in the extreme. It is very easy for the Cancer girl to marry, for her natural inclinations are so sympathetic that this quality of thought draws marriage to her. She seeks protection, and it always comes to her. But if she is a girl without a good deal of character and background, she will need the help and guidance of her husband for the strength to meet life's problems. Her husband is on a pedestal in her imagination, and if he fails her, the spiritual shock is crushing. When well aspected, the spiritual strength of the Cancer wife is as much a help to the husband as his worldly stamina is to her.

This native is passionately possessive and everything concerning the life of her family absorbs her completely. Sometimes these intuitive instinctive women have (counter to all else in their make up) an uncannily accurate business sense, and they are able to advise their husbands in business with unexpected wisdom. Taken generally, the whole character is proverbially feminine, and the man who marries a Cancer wife gets a completely womanly woman.

THE CANCER HUSBAND

June 22 to July 22

The Cancer husband is not an easy person to live with, despite the sign reputation for easy-going good nature.

The type is divided into at least two groups, one of which is the dominant. The husband of this group loves his home, but is exacting, fussy and inclined to be critical and fault-finding. The recessive Cancer man is so passive, lazy and self-indulgent that he often goes so far as to marry for money or position, in fact for any reason that will bring him ease, established position and domestic comfort. Since this kind of man is persistent and agreeable when he chooses to be, it is often possible for him to attain his ambition.

Any Cancer husband, whether of one type or another, spends more time in his home than other men. He has a deeply traditional love for the home and family, and has many of the same qualities in his nature that are imputed to the Cancer woman. The moodiness, changeability, sentimentality and effusiveness can be understood in a woman's nature, but translated to a man, these qualities are not inspiring, especially in large doses, administered domestically.

The Cancer husband means to be devoted, and his whole mind is wrapped up in his wife and family, but his disposition is such that these feelings are translated into exacting demands for service and constant interference in the home routine. Nothing satisfies him; he can always find something to criticize or complain about, and the most affectionate family feels the burden of this intensely possessive spirit. These men are very sensual and seek constant erotic stimulation. They are usually faithful enough, if their desires are satisfied at home. The effort entailed in conducting outside liaisons is too difficult for the Cancer man. He is rather timid, and abhors danger. Therefore while his senses might lead him astray, he is unwilling to be involved in complications that require effort to sustain.

THE LEO WIFE

July 23 to August 23

The Leo wife is a splendid type of woman for a worldly, ambitious man. She herself has an aristocratic point of view and all of the social graces. She is a great manager, and can run an elaborate home, take first place in the local social group, and advance her husband's business chances by enjoyable entertaining. She attracts people to her home and commands great respect. She is the sort of wife a husband wants his boss to meet, because the impression that she creates is helpful.

The love of a Leo wife is passionate, enduring, and self-sacrificing. These are the most loyal of women, whose whole lives are lived through their deep emotional natures. They give and feel, and bestow and bless. Their families can never show sufficient gratitude for the wealth of attention lavished upon them, and sometimes appear to lack appreciation for all this loving service. The truth is that no human being could repay the Leo wife's devotion to her home and husband. While her attitude is lush and generous in the extreme, unless the husband is a very dominant man, this type of wife will rule him, and the result will be a hen-pecked husband.

If the Leo woman is lucky enough to marry a virile, commanding man, all of her good qualities will be reduced to their rightful proportions. She will have the opportunity to exercise her housekeeping ability, lead the social group, and put all of her faith, and passionate love into her relationship with her husband. A supremely masculine man can supply her with the romantic outlets that her passionate nature requires, without sacrificing her femininity.

THE LEO HUSBAND

July 23 to August 23

The Leo man fits into the scheme of domestic life quite smoothly. Usually he is a good and very generous provider, desiring his wife and family to shine in the community. He is tremendously proud of not only them but himself, and he wants them to have the best of everything. For himself, he demands the center of the stage, and expects the home life to revolve around him, like planets around the sun. He is very affectionate, loving and devoted in his manner, but he will not tolerate disrespect or insubordination.

The Leo husband is fixed in his opinions about what is due him from wife and children. His love is deeply romantic, and very absorbing, but he considers that he is a law unto himself. Naturally very passionate, (although perfectly nor mal in his love nature), if he wishes to seek romantic adven ture outside of his home, he does so without scruple. But his attitude toward life is so conventional that he would never tolerate a wife who behaved in a similar manner. She must be above suspicion, and as the Leo men are acute judges of character, and fastidious to a fault, they usually select wives who meet with their high standards of perfection.

The average Leo man makes a fine husband. His generosity, kindness, loving disposition, and passionate loyalty in the big issues of life, plus his really great heart, make him a very safe and satisfying kind of husband for the feminine, clinging type of woman.

THE VIRGO WIFE

August 24 to September 23

Contrary to all the analysis of Virgo the woman, when she does marry she makes an excellent wife. That is, in certain respects. Her concept of marriage is the legal partnership idea, to be carried out as a smoothly-running business. She is usually capable, and arranges her housekeeping routine perfectly. The home is spotless, (everything seems to remain new), and the cooking excellent, She is vigilant and efficient—in fact she is everything that can make a home run like a well regulated machine. There is no such thing as waste or neglect in her home, for, the wife is, as they say, "on the job."

Her disposition is not so good. Perhaps all of this routine

is a strain, even when the nature is attuned to it. In any case, the Virgo wife is apt to be fussy, nagging, meticulous to a fault, and all of this regarding the most material matters, usually the running of this home that is nursed so tenderly. The Virgo wife guards the family purse jealously; in extreme cases she is very stingy, and in all of her responses to life she shows the same parsimonious attitude.

Emotionally this type of woman is often way below par. She responds to all of the outward routines of life, and meets traditional duties extraordinarily well. But the spiritual companionship and emotional ecstasy so necessary in a wife is more often than not entirely absent. She has in her make-up a selfish coldness that resents demands for more personal warmth; much as if such qualities, if she had them, would never be shared with anyone. It is doubtful if the Virgo wife ever recovers from her maiden beliefs that sex is base, and that she is descending when she accedes to her husband's physical necessities. A very clever man, who was deeply in love might alter this frame of mind, but since the Virgo woman seldom inspires that intensity of passion, her best hope is for a mate as restrained, practical and material as herself. In such an environment she makes a very successful wife.

THE VIRGO HUSBAND

August 24 to September 23

Almost the only kind of wife for the Virgo husband is the Virgo wife. These men are not interested in love in the passionate, personal, possessive sense of the term. They are usually conventional, traditionally-minded men, who accept domesticity because it is part of the social scheme. They are willing to conduct private life on a partnership basis, as if it were a commercial enterprise. In many cases they would prefer to be bachelors, and this sign does produce the bachelor by natural inclination. They are so abstemious that they cannot bear to indulge even themselves. Stinginess, a vice that has kept many a man from matrimony, is present in either a small or large degree in the Virgo nature.

As husbands, they are much like the women of the type. The high quality Virgoan is a capable man, making comfortable provision for his wife and family. If he is fussy, critical, peevish or complaining, (especially about health and expenses) he is also composed, kindly, thoughtful and conscientious. He safeguards his home and is careful to protect it from material disaster.

Unless there are other stimulating factors in the horoscope, the Virgo husband is not virile. He has little male dominance in his make-up, and is as loath to demand surrender as he is to give himself. He does not have a passionate urge, and his deepest approach to love is flirtation, or a play at love. Erotic flights of passion would never be attempted by him, and his point of view toward even average sexual performance is not enthusiastic.

THE LIBRA WIFE

September 24 to October 23

One of the most interesting love natures is found in either sex of the Libra person. The sign has a decided feminine leaning, with the highest Venus influence prevailing.

These women have a delicate, spiritual appeal. They are ideal wives for wealthy, successful men who are stimulated by union with a woman who is like an orchid. This type of wife looks exotic, and designs a background for herself in keeping with her rare, exquisite personality. Actually these women are not as fragile as they appear. The Libra wife is a fine mental companion, wise in the ways of partnership, and well able to bring harmony into the home life.

One of her special gifts is this talent for harmony. She has an instinctive knowledge of how to get along with people, and attracts an interesting social circle. At the same time she never neglects her own family, but gives them all the loving attention of which her gracious nature is capable.

The Libra wife is distinctly a luxury. She is usually very attractive, and always has a group of admirers seeking her favors. While she requires a varied social life, she is too well balanced to encourage indiscriminate flirtation, but if she were to find herself emotionally involved, her response would never be underhanded. This type of woman does not encourage scandal. Because she is so attractive, her life is sometimes more complicated than the existence of the plainer woman, but a husband can always feel confident that she will rise to the occasion.

As has been intimated, the Libra woman is the type who makes a lovely sheltered wife. Her passions are voluptuous, and demand a "quality setting." She is responsive, intuitive and intellectual. Her passional response to married life is extremely satisfying, and in many respects she is the best suited of all of the Zodiacal types to be a wife in the strictly personal sense of the word.

THE LIBRA HUSBAND

September 24 to October 23

The Libra husband is not an easy man to please. Temperamentally the sameness of domesticity is not to his liking, but he is a very passionate man, and a respecter of tradition, hence, marriage is the reasonable result. The Libra husband is reasonable; he is a born judge, and no other Zodiacal type can order the life with so much wisdom. His superior ability to guide the destiny of his home is one of his greatest virtues. Degenerate Libra characters do not have this power; they have the surface smoothness, but not the high intellectual development of which the best Libra men are capable. These men provide very well for their families, and seem to feel with the intensity of a woman the necessity of elegance and luxury in the home surroundings.

As has been said, the Libra husband is apt to be a very passionate man. His whole attitude toward love differs from the response made by the rest of the Zodiac. To the Libran, love is a high art. His passions are overwhelming, and he rises to great heights in the expressions of his love nature. This type of husband would be deeply disappointed if he did not meet with a satisfactory response to his passions. Even when the domestic partner is agreeable, he might be tempted to seek variety, but this is merely variety of expression. The Libra husband does not seek divorce, unless the conditions of his life are non-adjustable. He has an instinctive distrust of the untried, and will strain his judiciary talents guiding the domestic routine to satisfy his fastidious taste.

THE SCORPIO WIFE

October 24 to November 22

The Scorpio woman is a very primitive type, and her deepest feminine instincts are aroused by the different functions of being a wife. She takes marriage very seriously, and has an old-fashioned reverent attitude toward domestic responsibilities, as long as she is in love with her husband. Should this condition change, she follows without thought of consequences the dictates of her heart.

The best Scorpio wives are loyal and courageous, needing no hot-house atmosphere to keep their love in bloom. They enjoy responsibility, and a large family is a delight to them. These women are very capable, but once they are settled in domestic life they put all of the management and energy of their passionate natures into the home. They have the gift of home-making, and frequently organize a much better home than Cancer women or the Taurus women, who are famous for their instinct in home-making. The Scorpio woman loves luxury, and has considerable taste in house furnishings and the arrangement of the home.

The difference in the atmosphere of her surroundings lies in the intensity of her feelings. She is a blunt, fearless character, doing everything passionately from the depths of her being. Her devotion to her husband is whole-souled, but she does not idolize those she loves. Her reactions to life are intensely realistic, and she sees her man exactly as he is. Since she is neither shy, diffident or tactful she expresses herself with the greatest force. Her sexual appetite is large, and she requires vigorous satisfaction. The Scorpio person, man or woman, is inclined to excess, and while the moral sense rebels against the animal appetites, satisfaction usually comes first and repentance afterwards. It takes a very virile man, with a deep sympathy for sexual indulgence, to satisfy the Scorpio wife.

THE SCORPIO HUSBAND

October 24 to November 22

The Scorpio man makes one of the most difficult husbands to live with in peace and harmony. The only way that this can be accomplished is for the wife of a Scorpio man to be receptive to his every thought and follow his instructions with complete obedience. He is the typical "old fashioned lord of the manor" and is just as tyrannical and overbearing in his home as he is in every other walk of life.

Many astrological warnings have been given against marriage for the Scorpio man with afflictions in his seventh house of marriage. He is considered too extreme in his reactions to the love life. But the temperament is such that no matter how forewarned, these men will marry, and tragedy is too often the result.

For the less extreme types there are more chances of happiness. The Scorpio man himself is often very successful, and well able to support a wife and the large family he so desires. But his intensely personal passions, and the highly possessive attitude of his devotion is a strain on the most devoted family. In fact, no matter how much love and attention he receives, his nature is secretive and suspicious, and he will always suspect deceptive conditions working against him. These conditions are wholly imaginative, but he persists in inflaming himself with jealousy and dark inward resentments.

The depths of his affection for the wife and children are genuine indeed, but he cannot seem to learn to be more pliable. Such selfish love is bound to cheat itself as the unhappy Scorpio man makes his stubborn way through life.

Sexual excesses are often a part of this sign character. The desires are gross and unnatural, and demand satisfaction. As is the case with the women of the sign, Scorpio men have a strong moral side to the character. They suffer deeply for their indulgences, and make inward promises of temperance after the appetites have been satisfied.

THE SAGITTARIAN WIFE

November 23 to December 21

The Sagittarian wife is the best fitted of all Zodiacal types to be a companion to her husband. This type of woman takes an intelligent interest in her husband's business. She is not an intruder and has enough reserve to wait until she is asked for advice, but when the confidences come, she is not only a sympathetic listener but a useful adviser.

In the field of hobbies and sports she is a real pal. All outdoor life attracts her, and she enjoys fishing, hunting, riding and even the competitive sports. A man does not have to search for a companion to enjoy his hobby with him if he is married to a Sagittarian woman. She is enthusiastic about all kinds of activity, civic affairs, social life, sportsmanship, club life, and intellectual advancement; and she even enjoys a fling at gambling. It is easy to see that a husband can have a very full life with such a companion.

In the home, this kind of wife is competent, speedy in her

housekeeping, efficient and sympathetic in the care of her children, very clever and well balanced in all of her reactions to life. She is a woman to be trusted, for her judgments are mature, and her natural mental equipment sound.

A good percentage of athletic beauty goes with this birth position, and these women are often tall, handsome and smartly gowned. They demand an active life, for there is nothing of the languid hothouse bloom about them. There is no petty jealousy in their make-up either, and though they seek a wide circle of friends of both sexes, they are canny enough to know how to avoid emotional complications. They seldom embarrass the husband with nagging suspicions, and are quite apt to treat his passing preferences with tactful oversight.

These wives are not so tactful about the more everyday faults of living. They are outspoken in the extreme, and both the husband and the children may expect to hear their errors frankly discussed, very often for their own good.

The emotional nature of the Sagittarian woman is highly nervous. Her passions are healthy, joyous and swift. She does not make a fetish of physical indulgence, but she is rather highly sexed and demands stimulating, adventurous excitement. Her responses are enthusiastic, and her approach to physical love highly refined and inspiring.

THE SAGITTARIAN HUSBAND

November 23 to December 21

The Sagittarian husband requires a wise, tactful wife. This may be true of all husbands, but the men born with this birth figure have much to give, and frequently the family, because they will not cater to innate peculiarities, see the worst side of the character, rather than the best, which is so good.

This type of man is not ideally fitted by nature for domestic life. His interests in world affairs are great, and his profession or business is usually chosen from the depths of these interests. He loves humanity, and takes an absorbing interest in social progress, and the practical problems that confront his world, or his community. He is very much of a public man. His basic mental strength goes into life in general so that life in particular—that is his personal life—becomes small, childish and unimportant by comparison.

If his personal tastes change, he sees no reason why he must continue to express a devotion that no longer exists, and since love is like a rather sportive game to him, he can see no special wrong in his change of preference.

Of course this is hard on married life, where singleness of thought is the ideal, and anything less stable makes for constant friction. The wife of this type of man had best be exceedingly broad-minded, free from jealousy, and impersonal, even if this is not natural to her. She will have to be a good deal of an actress to hold his interest in any case.

This is not meant to imply that the Sagittarian man does not stay married, or that he does not make a good husband. On the contrary, these are very gifted men, with whom it is a privilege to live. But because of their lack of the personal sense, and their impatience with anything narrow or ordered in the life, it is necessary for a wife of such a man to widen her own horizon so that she may see eye to eye with her husband.

The passions of the Sagittarian are lusty, sportive, and adventurous. They are joyous fellows, and they treat love like a happy adventure. All of the emotions accompanying this birth figure are nervous and high-strung, and demand immediate satisfaction.

THE CAPRICORN WIFE

December 22 to January 19

The sign of Capricorn does not favor women. That is, not in the sense of creating a womanly woman, intuitive, sensitive, variable, and spiritual. The Capricorn woman is rather masculine in her appearance, and in her temperament as well. She is capable, faithful, dependable and systematic.

Household routine is a joy to her, and she is one of the finest housekeepers of all of the Zodiacal types. She is a cook, she is an economist, she is somewhat of a hostess, and she is very ambitious for her husband's and children's success in the world.

With all of these necessary virtues brought to such a high scale of perfection, it is somewhat odd that the Capricorn wife is not advertised from the housetops as being the ideal of wives.

What the Capricorn female personality lacks is the soft feminine sympathy, the pliant submissiveness, and the physical responsiveness of the Libra or the Pisces woman. The emotional generosity of the Aries or the Leo woman is absent. Even the hearty comradeship of the Sagittarian woman is not there. In its place, we find the efficient trained housekeeper, scrupulous in her integrity, and a slave to her duty. Many men prefer less perfection and more warmth.

In many ways this is all very unfair to the Capricorn wife. She is really an admirable kind of woman, needing, most of all, encouragement and affection to call forth all of her deep loyalty, which once given, lasts a lifetime.

Men of a more serious practical nature, who do not seek spiritual or emotional companionship from their wives but wish their home life to run along smoothly, rather like a high-class hotel, will find this type of wife very satisfactory.

THE CAPRICORN HUSBAND

December 22 to January 19

The Capricorn husband falls in readily enough with the domestic scheme, but adds little to its spiritual success. This type of man usually marries, but his reasons are supremely selfish. Of course selfishness has been ascribed to plenty of other kinds of men, but the basic nature of Capricorn is selfish.

As husbands, these men are good providers, for they are ambitious and successful in business most of the time. They do not allow much freedom of action to their wives, so that even if there is plenty of money in the home, the wife is not free to spend it. A Capricorn husband is very dictatorial as well as conservative, and lays down hard and fast rules for the spending of his money. In fact, the entire household is directed by this type of husband, to whom his wife is a lieutenant. As a commanding officer he is exacting, tyrannical, obstinate, and unreasonable, laying down laws for the family routine that may be in accordance with good discipline, but wholly unsympathetic to a happy home.

He is generally not a good emotional companion for his wife, having neither the ability nor the willingness to give even a part of himself to create an atmosphere of enjoyment, much less to add to the real pleasure of the moment. He demands that everything be given to him, and examines whatever he gets with caution and suspicion. He would never believe that some contribution from himself was necessary to heighten his own enjoyment, and he would never be willing to give of himself even if convinced. His passions are strong but quick, and he considers them entirely animal, to be satisfied and disposed of without development or delicacy.

Naturally the harsh tone that this birth figure casts over a personality is usually tempered by the other configurations. In that case many of the sober Capricorn qualities are embellished by softer moods, making, of course, a much more agreeable person.

THE AQUARIAN WIFE

January 20 to February 18

The Aquarian woman is one of the highest of the Zodiacal types, but she does not slip into matrimony with the ease of a sensitive little Cancer woman, or an insinuating Pisces woman, and yet the Aquarian woman is better equipped for marriage than either of the two types mentioned.

She is better equipped in that she is a capable, intellectual woman, discerning, adaptable, and often very talented. She has a man's ability to accomplish a day's work without grumbling or fatigue, and coupled with her undoubted ability to be a good housekeeper, she is, like the Sagittarian woman, a very fine companion.

She attracts people, and her easy, friendly manners make her home a social center. Her interests are apt to be wide, and it never occurs to her to watch the husband's actions with suspicion, or try to check up on how he spends his spare time. Naturally, she trusts him. Her own behavior is above reproach. Aquarian women are the kindest in the world, and they would rather suffer themselves than create a condition from which some one else might have grief and sorrow. However, basically, the Aquarian woman is unconventional, and should her urge for a change of partners be sufficiently justified, she would make the change.

Emotionally, she is responsive, but her intellect rules her, and she is the most appreciated as a wife when married to an intellectual man, whose work she can share, and who is able to use her undoubted abilities in his own behalf.

THE AQUARIAN HUSBAND

January 20 to February 18

The Aquarian husband is the kindest and most generous of all the types. The generosity of the Leo man and even the Aries man is advertised, but it is oppressive compared to the open-handed spirit, the giving without thought of return or reward that is part of the character of the Aquarian husband.

Aquarian men are not ardent lovers; that is, not unless some other planetary configurations stimulate this urge. But, since they are gracious, social, kindly people they accept marriage as part of the domestic scheme, and cooperative as they are, make a great success of it. Their success consists of their own attitude, which contributes a great deal toward harmony in the home.

They are considerate men, perfect gentlemen in every way, treating their wives and family with the same consideration and courtesy that they accord to strangers.

The drawback in their marital relationship appears to be their impersonality. Women seem to prefer the possessive, somewhat selfish dominance of the more personal types to the broadminded attitude of the Aquarian husband. His impersonality appears to many women like lack of interest, and, as self-centered wives, they want the whole attention of their husband. It has been said that the Aquarians' universal interest, will one day be the attitude of the entire world, but in the meantime, the domestic life of such men will be far more successful if married to a highly intellectual woman, whose work in the world is as important as their own broad interests.

THE PISCES WIFE

February 19 to March 20

The Pisces woman is ideally adapted for the domestic life. She is not as active as many of the other types, or as capable, but her spiritual qualities and emotional responses far outclass most of the other Zodiacal types. For this reason, many men might be willing to sacrifice personal comfort, for the spiritual and emotional escape provided by the companionship of this type of woman.

Not that the Pisces woman is incompetent, for she herself has a great sense of comfort, and is thoughtful of others, studying the home so that it will be a restful, luxurious place of refuge. But very often she has not the energy or the practicality to carry out her good intentions.

If the Pisces wife should be of the self-indulgent type, beautiful perhaps, and talented, she may dream away the days, idly seeking entertainment, or what is more dangerous, erotic, sensational pleasures which she fancies can be found among spiritualistic mediums, and faddy religious cults. The very worst results come from indulgences of this kind.

Sometimes the health of the Pisces wife is delicate, and then it takes the utmost strength of will to keep her optimistic and wholesome mentally.

This negative side of the sensitive Pisces nature is not inviting, but when the type is more robust, the women make the kindest, most loving, devoted and sympathetic of wives. They are extremely responsive, and this tends to make them very good mates in the physical sense of the word. They are adaptable and experimental, and their concept of sex is high and beautiful, far above the average.

THE PISCES HUSBAND

February 19 to March 20

The Pisces husband is full of doubtful benefits to the home and wife. He is one of the most loving and attentive of men, considerate, thoughtful, the eternal escort, showering his wife with courtesy.

He spends more time in the home than any other type, save perhaps the Cancer husband, but he is not a good provider, and although he goes through the motions of giving to his wife, he often has nothing material to give. And what is worse, it is impossible to arouse him to a sense of reality. This sense of reality, overdone with several of the other signs, is entirely lacking in the Piscean. His notions, dreams and misconceptions are more real to him than the difficulties of living, which are almost impossible to conquer, and therefore immediately substituted by him for a phantom world.

These qualities in a husband are most distressing, especially with the struggle for existence staring the household in the face. Naturally every Piscean husband is not incompetent, as other aspects in the birth figure help to build up the personal energy. The main fault with this configuration for the husband is that it lacks stability, strength, and realism, all of those qualities so necessary for the family provider. If this type of man happens to have sufficient direction in his nature to guide him to the kind of work for which he is best suited, and he has the fight to persist until he is successful, he will then make a very good husband, since the softer qualities are so dominant in his nature.

The Pisces husband is very sensual, and seeks a sympathetic response to his physical nature. The call of his senses can be dangerously perverted by self-indulgence; or he may be just highly sexed, according to other figures in the birth scheme. In any case, he is the type of man to whom sexual satisfaction is important, and he seeks it persistently all of his life.

GUIDE FOR PARENTS

1. *THE PARENTS*

Most people are parents at some time during their adult life. It is one of the great responsibilities that are of our own making regardless of whether we are fitted for the duty or not.

A great many rules have been made regarding how children should treat parents, not omitting the illustrious mandate of the Ten Commandments, "Honor thy father and mother, as the Lord thy God hath commanded thee; that thy days may be prolonged, and that it may go well with thee, in the land which the Lord thy God giveth thee."

Since the majority has always ruled, it seems quite natural that there should be many sacred admonitions for the behavior of children to parents, but the world is beginning to take into account how badly equipped most of us are to be parents. We are beginning to learn how little we understand the delicate nature of the child, and how much damage we do to the growing personality that, with intelligent preparation, might be better equipped to face the struggle for existence. It is not so much the smoothing of the path for our children that is important, but the strengthening of them, that they may smooth the path for themselves.

It has been said that "The Way Of All Flesh" by Samuel Butler was the first English novel ever written that denied the perfection of parents. The book is a classic on the mismanagement of the English children of past centuries, but happily those conditions have been swept away. In America, the study and development of our children has always been recognized for their value to the future of our country, as well as for the good hearted kindness so much a part of the American people.

Among the astrological types, some of us are naturally suited to be parents, and some of us, once we know wherein we fail, can invoke the improvements by ourselves.

THE ARIES PARENT

The Aries parent (March 21 to April 19) of either sex is kind and generous to children, but not always sympathetic or understanding. This is particularly true of the Aries father, who, while he is proud of his children, is apt to be impatient and irritable, and unwilling to see their problems through their eyes.

The Aries mother is a somewhat different personality. She too is intensely proud of her children, and apt to be somewhat unconventional and advanced in her methods of rearing them. She may urge them to use their own judgment a good deal more than is permitted to most children, and of course it depends upon the astrological group of her child whether this is a good thing or not. Since the inherited pattern does enter into the matter, the chances are that the child will have considerable of the mother's initiative. In any case it is always well to encourage a child to develop judgment and taste. On the whole, barring impatience, the Aries parents, particularly the Aries mother, are fairly efficient and a good example of independence and courage to the growing child.

THE TAURUS PARENT

The Taurus parent (April 20 to May 20) of either sex is often considered one of the ideal types of parent. They have endless patience, a natural love for children and the home life, which so often revolves around the youngsters in the family. This routine is not boring to the Taurean, as it is to so many of the other Zodiacal types. Taureans almost always choose country life, or at least suburban life, which is ideal for the growing family. Parents of this group have a very protective instinct, and while they are seldom brilliant intellectual people themselves, their kindness of heart and common sense as well as strongly intuitive qualities go a long way toward giving a child the kind of guidance most needed.

THE GEMINI PARENT

The Gemini person (May 21 to June 21) of either sex does not make an ideal parent. There is too much mind, and not enough heart in the make-up to be effective with children. These people have a youthful outlook themselves, and a fresh and lively point of view. This may help them to understand their children, although it is not necessary to be like a child to understand children. A good memory will serve as well. The Gemini person must cultivate patience and affection, and try to create a restful atmosphere in the home rather than a stimulating or exciting one. The Gemini person's whole reaction to life lacks warmth and affection, but this is particularly important in the relationship with children. There are many problems that pure reason alone will not solve, and one of them is the guidance of children. It is a fine thing for children to have intellectual parents, if the par-

ents give the children a chance to absorb some of this mental
activity and begin to put it to use early in the life.

THE CANCER PARENT

The Cancer person (June 22 to July 22) has been described as the personification of motherhood. It is true that
these people love children, and make the greatest amount of
fuss over them. But they are not always wise in rearing them.
The Cancer father is exacting, fussy and critical; and super-
vises his children until they become nervous and self-con-
scious. The Cancer mother dotes on them until they become
naughty, and then she rebukes them too sternly. She herself
is full of tempers, and has very little control over her own
emotions; consequently her discipline is too severe. She is
the sort of parent who is both too easy and too hard. The
child never knows what is going to happen, and soon learns
that there is very little justice in his or her young life. These
parents give plenty of love, but their attitude is not sufficiently reasonable for the guidance of children, and though
they are very devoted parents the atmosphere is too hysteri-
cal for complete success.

THE LEO PARENT

The Leo person (July 23 to August 23) of both sexes
makes, on general principles, a rather good parent. The Leo
mother is particularly successful. She is a little too dictatorial and dominant, but her love is so sincere that her children soon realize its strength. She is very ambitious, and
manages to procure for them every possible advantage. Perhaps the greatest fault of parents of both sexes in the Leo
sign is the desire to rule absolutely over the home as if it
were a kingdom. Either the ruler demands too much attention, or smothers the children with attention, making them
too dependent on the advantages that they receive in the
home. There is no doubt about the generosity and quality
of the Leo love for their children, for it ranks first of all in

the emotional responses to children from the twelve signs of the Zodiac.

THE VIRGO PARENT

The Virgo person (August 24 to September 23) makes an excellent parent; that is, so far as the visual and material factors in the life are concerned. The Virgo mother notices everything. She is meticulous about her children's appearance, and instills into them very early in life a sense of method and order. She watches their manners, morals and advancement in school with the greatest care, and no social position matters to her as much as her children's progress. She trains them to be a help to themselves. The Virgo father has much the same attitude as the Virgo mother, and the most serious fault of both sexes as parents is too much supervision and nagging.

THE LIBRA PARENT

The Libra parent (September 24 to October 23) is one of the best parents of the Zodiac. Whether it be the mother or father who is a Libra person, they seem to have an instinctive understanding of children. They radiate a gentle comradeship that guides and instructs without too restraining a hand. The Libra parent seems to have the gift for making a child enjoy instruction. They show their love and devotion for their youngsters by a really intelligent direction of development, which is neither tyrannical nor too indulgent. In parents the Libra qualities of judgment and balance are used to the greatest advantage.

THE SCORPIO PARENT

The Scorpio parent (October 24 to November 22) is, alas! one of the most prolific types, and the poorest-equipped to bring up children. They (both sexes) are impatient, ambitious, tyrannical and severe. Their devotion to their children is boundless, but their behavior lacks common sense and control. They are often harsh, and their methods of discipline too severe. Despite the fact that Scorpio people are very wise and have an intuitive knowledge of life, they are too much the slave of their passions to put into practice the restrained common sense so necessary to the guidance of children. The Scorpio parents must learn to harness their passions and serve their children, giving them the benefit of their own natural gifts. Otherwise the offspring of such a home environment will grow up too weak-kneed and cowed to fight the ordinary battles of life, to say nothing of their inward and secret resentment against the parents.

THE SAGITTARIAN PARENT

The Sagittarian (November 23 to December 21) woman, makes a better parent than the Sagittarian man. As a father, the Sagittarian is not sufficiently detailed in the supervision of his children, and he appears to be disinterested. It has been said that these people have such a great interest in the world at large that it would not be asking too much to designate a better proportion to the children of the native. The Sagittarian has so much to give that his impatience with his own family often robs them of the benefits he bestows on the outside world. The Sagittarian woman serves her children with much more specialized attention than the Sagittarian man. In fact, she has some of the Libra person's good sense in the rearing of her children, and in addition often inculcates them very early in life with an interest in world affairs, national problems, and a philosophical approach to religion. This is rather advanced food for children, but the children of intellectual parents soon learn that higher thought is everyday fare.

THE CAPRICORN PARENT

The Capricorn mother (December 22 to January 19) is a far better parent than the Capricorn father. This type of mother is rather like the Virgo mother in her detailed supervision of her children and her persistent efforts to raise the standard of the child's school work and general behavior. Like the Virgo mother, she sometimes errs on the side of commission rather than omission. She is exceedingly ambitious, and may in her zeal for progress push her children beyond their capabilities. The Capricorn father is far too exacting and severe. He resembles the Scorpio parent in that he has no patience with the weaknesses of childhood, and judges children by adult standards. He is harsh and unsympathetic, and thinks only in terms of discipline. Relaxation and pleasure have little place in his own program, and he sees no need to supply his children with enjoyment, which he thinks of as self-indulgence. This type of parent dominated by the planet Saturn as he is, can expect little but fear from his children. Unless he tempers his severity, he will lose out in the most satisfactory emotional returns obtainable by everyone who is a parent; that is, he may forfeit the love of his children.

THE AQUARIAN PARENT

The Aquarian parent (January 20 to February 18) of both sexes makes the ideal parent. Aquarius is the human sign, and the qualities dominant in the sign-character are ideal for the development of children. These people can guide and encourage children, spurring them on to excel, without boastfulness. The Aquarian can instil in his or her children respect for the parents' judgment. Children of Aquarian parents will ask advice fearlessly, knowing that they will never be unduly censured for possible mistakes. The Aquarian method of rearing children is kind guidance and reasonable correction. These parents make every effort to engage the child's real interest in studies and advancement, not merely stimulate his or her competitive spirit. Children of this type of parents are treated with great affection, but never mauled, devoured, or deluged with sentimentality. The Aquarian always tries to create mental appreciation, believ-

ing that this will endure long after the emotional effusions
are spent.

THE PISCEAN PARENT

The Sign of Pisces is a very fertile sign (February 19 to
March 20). These people (both sexes) make loving and devoted parents, but they are apt to be too indulgent for the
good of their children. The highly developed Piscean lives
such a remote spiritual, existence that the practical but delicate problem of child training eludes him. For the most part,
this is too hard a job for Pisceans to work at seriously and
consistently. These people, because of their deep love for
their children, believe that is sufficient in its spiritual sig-
nificance for guidance. While the value of unseen forces is
an interesting debatable point, the growing children surrounding the parents need direction of a more tangible sort.
The Pisces parents enjoy the companionship of the children,
and are one with them in many ways, but the hard work of
supervision is something that they try to avoid simply by
letting the child have his or her own way. Parents of this
group might try to discipline themselves to the point where
the less agreeable duties of child development are as faith-
fully undertaken by them as they, in their imagination, believe. The Pisces person is seldom aware of shortcomings,
and usually judges results by the perfection of the spiritual
visions.

2. *THE CHILDREN*

The following pages offer a record, as far as it is possible
to record anything so delicate as a child's character, of the
children of the Zodiac.

During the early years of the child's life, the influence of
the planetary nativity is quite strong. The experiences of
life, plus the progression of heavenly transits, have not had
a chance to alter the original pattern. Therefore this brief

review will give the parent some idea of the child's fundamental make-up, which, as well as the parent may know the child, will be helpfully revealing.

THE CHILD OF ARIES
March 21 to April 20

The child of Aries is the most precocious and brilliant child of all twelve of the sign-characters.

These children often show the beginning of several talents, which if encouraged and developed from the start, (instead of exploited), may foster a creative trend that will be valuable by the time they are of a suitable age for advanced work.

Aries children should not be encouraged to show off. The pleasant aura of adult attention causes them to display their talents too freely, and to tell exaggerated stories. If they are too harshly reprimanded, it will hurt their pride, which is very strong. Yet a gentle restraint must be used. First, keep exhibitions of their marked ability strictly among competitive groups of gifted children. They must never compete with adults, no matter how high the standard of juvenile talent. The second problem is to impress the importance of accuracy in narration. Imaginative children, such as these are, have a tendency to "build things up." Try to teach them that a good story is interesting enough without embellishment, and the best story is the simplest. The point is that children will not continue to tell untruths when they are positive that there is absolutely nothing to fear.

A certain amount of freedom will do this type of child good. They like to try their own wings, and they resent too much supervision. If only for the mistakes that they will make, and the resulting lessons, they should be encouraged at times to guide themselves.

The parent of this child must develop rather than exploit the talents. There is so wide a range in Aries groups between the noble and the inferior that the parent has plenty of material but a difficult task.

THE CHILD OF TAURUS

April 20 to May 21

The Taurus child is one of the most beautiful children of the twelve types. They are usually well-grown, developed, sturdy and healthy in appearance. They eat well and have plenty of energy and vitality.

These children respond to love and affection, and crave a great deal of petting. They appear to be rather stolid, but this is really shyness, and if they are properly encouraged to be friendly, the timidity vanishes.

Taurus is not an intellectual sign, and these are not studious children. They must be encouraged to study. Sometimes they show an aptitude toward manual work with a distinctly artistic trend, and this should be encouraged, with a moderate amount of mental training. But regardless of what engages them, they must very early in life have instilled into the consciousness of a love for application. These children can easily become lazy, as the sign-character leans toward self-indulgence. Good, helpful friendships with other children should be encouraged. The Taurus child could, through love of pleasure, choose companions that might stimulate the lackadaisical, idle habits lying dormant in the nature. Therefore intelligent supervision of companions is a necessity.

Gentle interest and quiet stimulation will bring to life all of the fine qualities, and ability to accomplish that later in life is a part of the Taurus character.

THE CHILD OF GEMINI

May 21 to June 21

The Gemini child is like the dual sign, both a blessing and a problem. They are talented youngsters, often showing very young, ability to draw, dance, or play musical instruments. They do well in school, and have a natural aptitude for their studies. Teachers are satisfied, and the child presents no problem as long as his or her mind is occupied in school.

The Gemini child's weaknesses are those of disposition. They are nervous, high-strung children who find it hard to capture repose. It is difficult for them to rest or sleep, and both are necessary for the health and well-being of the child.

They are great little exaggerators and story-tellers. Actually they themselves do not know where fact begins and fancy ends. They love acting, masquerading and all sorts of drama. It is wise for the parent to encourage play-acting, and to make clear at the same time that exaggerated story-telling belongs to the fairy tale world, and is distinctly an amusement, but has no part at all in the world of reality.

Also, the desire to chatter, so stimulating to these nervous children, had best be quietly curbed. This excited talk may appear "cute" in the tot, but later in the life may develop into the practice of dangerous gossiping.

The Gemini child wearies of everything, and some effort should be made by the parent to develop appreciation of its property and possessions.

If this child is not affectionate, this can be overcome by tenderness and loving demonstrations from the parent to the child.

THE CHILD OF CANCER

June 22 to July 23

Cancer children are sensitive plants. More often than not they have none of the graces found in some of the other signs. They are not clever, talented in a flashy way, studious, or even very robust. They are fanciful, moody, clinging little things, hungering for love and understanding. They get strange passionate attachments for people and absorb almost anything that attracts them.

In order to bring the Cancer child up to a more active, open, normal outlook, the parent must be very loving and attentive, but must manage in some way to make the child more independent and outspoken. These children must actually be made to like to do things for themselves. Since the ability to absorb and imitate is so strong, the examples set for them should be of activity, ambition and accomplishment.

They are not studious or intellectual in any way, but manual dexterity and business ability are part of the natural Cancer make-up, and can by cultivation be brought out in these children. As has been stressed, almost any quality can be developed in these children that is within their scope.

The health of this type of child is exceedingly delicate. The appetite is poor, and the very foods that are worst for them are likely to attract them the most. Naturally, the light, simple, nourishing diet is ideal. It is hard to build these children up, partly because their resistance is low, but mainly because their physical delicacy makes them susceptible to so many illnesses. A happy life in the country, gentle young companions, and a routine, well divided among school, rest and play is what the Cancer child needs for the best development.

THE CHILD OF LEO

July 23 to August 23

The Leo children are the most vital and active of all the types. They are highly strung, domineering, and much inclined to show off. Actually they are often handsome, lovable children, full of talent. They excel in outdoor sports, and are healthy, tireless and able to compete successfully in any field where children are the contenders. Naturally, with all of these virtues, unrestrained, they lose their balance and show traits that, if allowed to develop, will make them objectionable adults. They are much too bossy, and should not be allowed to indulge their desire for boasting and self-praise.

It must be brought home to them that good work, well

done, will sooner or later cause the proper amount of admiration, which is not nearly so important as proficiency, which is what really makes a worth-while character. Praise comes as a result of work well done, but the thrill should come from accomplishment and not from applause. The Leo child is very intelligent and will readily learn all the good things that he or she is taught. In fact they are strongly idealistic and crave instruction; and like to have an example set for them by someone whom they admire.

This is one child who offers a rich nature of good impulses, but because of the vast amount of energy, it needs very careful direction.

THE CHILD OF VIRGO

August 23 to September 23

Virgo children are one of the most mental types of all twelve signs. They are admirable students, and love their school work because of the natural intellectual curiosity in their make-up. They are perpetually in a state of inquiry, and scarcely any other type of child asks why and how and when so frequently. They are apt to excel in their school work, and respond to special training in many of the special fields of science, mathematics and the graphic arts.

As with the Gemini children, the parents' special problem is in the disposition of the child. They have an urge toward perfection, but in the search they become cross, peevish, fault-finding, critical and irritable. The basis of all this is an inherent lack of warmth and a coldness toward humanity. The wise parent will be very affectionate to these children in a manner that is not too physical. They have a misconception of physical caress, and think of this type of warmth as animalistic. They must learn that gentle, tender caresses are the natural human expression of love.

A pleasant social life should be encouraged for the Virgo

child, and the parents might encourage plenty of little visitors in the home. The disposition of these children is too cold, and they do not make friends. If sociability and generosity are encouraged early in the life, much of this squeamishness and fuss-budget selfishness will disappear from the nature by the time the child is grown to manhood or womanhood.

The Child of Libra

September 23 to October 24

Libra children are not simple personalities to develop. They are sympathetic children, both clinging and reserved. They respond to affection shyly, and yet in their inner natures they crave love. They want to respond, but have so much restraint that it is hard for them to relax. The special work of the parent with this type of child is to teach it to unfold.

They have good mentality, intellectual leanings, and very often marked artistic talents along the lines of painting, drawing, music, dancing or acting. But with all of these possibilities, they have apathetic dispositions and no energy or personal urge to develop any part of their capabilities themselves. They are supremely unambitious. The parent must seek out the bent, and very early in the life develop ambition and the ability to get ahead. For without the cultivation of direction in the life, this type of child will grow up frittering away the talents without the stability or will-power to succeed.

As the child approaches the teens, another problem is faced by the parents. These children are so responsive and delicately tuned to the physical urges, that they are likely to experiment too deeply to discover the sources and results of these sensations that give them so much delight. They are very self-indulgent, and place no moral valuation upon sexual experiments. It might be advisable to be clear and open in talking to the adolescent of Libra upon the value of the proper time and place for sex in the life of an adult.

A good deal of responsibility rests with the parents in what kind of a person their Libra child will grow up to be, and while this is true of all children, the Libra child, as can plainly be seen from this characterization, presents some especially delicate problems.

THE CHILD OF SCORPIO

October 24 to November 23

Scorpio children are one of the most active and energetic of all of the twelve types. They have good minds, naturally keen and comprehensive, and are able to grasp their studies without difficulty. In fact, they revel in problems, and cheerfully go to the heart of any work detailed to them. They attack everything with gusto, and the danger is that they will not find enough activity in the life for their boundless energy. Their capacity for work is tremendous, and their nature is rich in avenues for development.

The difficulties facing parents in the development of these children are faults of character. The Scorpio child is often underhanded and deceitful. If he cannot get his own way by fair means, he will attempt the foul. He is not penitent under rebuke, but sullen and resentful. This type will even go so far as to pretend sorrow over their misdeeds, but in reality the faults continue behind the parents' back. Selfishness and self-indulgence are strong in the Scorpio child's nature, and it can be seen that the parents of these children have their hands full to combat the evils lying dormant in the nature. If the parent does his or her work well, the child when grown up will have a happier life. Scorpio people always suffer cruelly in one way or another from their vices. Either their conscience plagues them, or some other retribution overtakes them. It will be a blessing to the child if the parent forces all of these hidden wrongs, such as sexual indulgence, private bullying of other children, and all forms of deceitfulness out into the open. Any fault in a child that is faced fearlessly can be successfully conquered.

THE CHILD OF SAGITTARIUS

November 23 to December 22

This type of child is usually a joy to the parents. They are happy, cheerful and optimistic, with a natural tendency toward good behavior. It is the rule rather than the exception for the Sagittarian child to choose the right rather than the wrong way to do things. Their fundamental ethics are sound, and they do not deceive or misrepresent. They are kind, loving, friendly, and consequently popular. They are apt at their studies, and enjoy leadership without lording it over their companions. They are so trusting and unselfish that sometimes it is wise for the parent to teach this type of child to examine motives and personality more specifically. Everyone is not good, and the Sagittarian all through the life suffers from an excess of trust in mankind.

The special problem of the parents here is to direct this valuable energy. The Sagittarian child rebels against control, is willful, and tries to throw off authority. Many as are their capabilities and virtues, they are not responsible, nor are they even able to take care of themselves, as they so fondly believe.

Wherever it is possible, it will do them good to be allowed freedom of action. They love sports and animals, and should be encouraged to take up what ever kind of athletics they choose, as well as to have as many pets as circumstances will allow.

But where choosing friends and occupations is concerned, the help and guidance of the father and mother are essential.

THE CHILD OF CAPRICORN

December 22 to January 21

The child of Capricorn is the type of which we often hear people say that he or she "was an old-fashioned little thing." That is one of the principal failings of Capricorn children. They are mature for their ages, solemn, repressed and unresponsive. It is not natural or good for a child to be anything but joyous and carefree, and everything should be done by the parents to lighten the darkness of this temperament.

These children are rather slow in their mental responses, but they are exceedingly painstaking and persevering. As a result they often succeed, especially in their school work, where more brilliant children fail. In fact, their average of studious accomplishment is very high. They have an innate respect for learning, and are surprisingly ambitious. Scholarship is not lost upon them, and they put education to good use.

They have not naturally sweet dispositions, and parents will have to work very hard to eradicate tendencies toward deceit, schemes and spitefulness. It is disappointing to find these qualities in a child, when they are hateful enough in adults. Parents, if they detect such tendencies, will have to treat them like a physical illness, and slowly and patiently develop trust and sweetness and sociability in their stead. These children are great readers and through the direction of the reading much salvation can be accomplished. If the realistic nature is apt to be too sordid, idealism, human kindness and spirituality can be developed by study of the noblest literature. It will take patience; but what are parents for but to study and guide their children?

THE CHILD OF AQUARIUS

January 21 to February 20

Aquarian children are very promising in many ways. They are not brilliant students, and book-learning along

routine lines burdens them. But they have a great interest
in progressive accomplishment, the progress of the world,
or even of the small community in which they live, which
is remarkable in a child who is more apt to be self-centered,
and thinks only of his or her own small pleasures. The
Aquarian youngster is very different, in that a child of either
sex, but especially the boys, has a distinctly humanitarian
trend. They want to serve in a big way, and think very
little about themselves. This urge often produces a genius
in one way or another.

The duty of the parents in this case is to make formal education attractive. If a person is to be a great success in the
world to-day, and offer the service that most Aquarians wish
to give, it is necessary to start out with at least the same advantages enjoyed by everyone else. Since a college education
or its equivalent is quite general, the Aquarian child should
be induced to see the advantage of it, and since these are
the most reasonable of all children, and the most sincere
in their efforts for advancement, they will accept all of the
school training that the parent thinks is necessary. In most
cases everything that the parent expends on the Aquarian
son or daughter is well repaid. Aquarian children have a
strong sense of obligation, and exert themselves to be worthy
of trust.

These children should be guided to keep promises and
avoid delays. They are so enthusiastic that they often promise what they cannot fulfill. Later in life, (if this habit develops), they get a reputation for exaggeration and are not
believed even when they are telling the truth. As children
they procrastinate, and put off unpleasant duties from day
to day. This is perhaps a general fault with most types, but
in the Aquarian, extreme good nature gives them a tendency
to be too lax. When they grow up, their work in the world
is often important, and even small weaknesses in a great
character become a target for enemies.

The parents of the Aquarian child often have in their

hands a potential genius, or at least a public benefactor, and it is advisable to study the inclinations of the child with the greatest care.

THE CHILD OF PISCES

February 20 to March 21

The Pisces child has great potentialities for good. They are deeply spiritual children, always wishing for the perfect and the beautiful, and living, alas, too much in dreams and fancies. They have little sense of realism and have no idea of what the world is like, or what it expects of them in the way of accomplishment.

They are often talented, especially in music, designing and painting, poetry and prose, but they lack self-confidence, and they have not the urge of the creator to develop their work and put it before the world. They enjoy reading and studies, but are shy, secretive, and timid about taking an oral part in school discussions. They have no confidence in their own ability, and when doing their work, if it is difficult, they want to throw it aside for fear that they will not succeed. They are always certain that they cannot compete with others, and shrink from the pain of failure; consequently they had much rather not try at all.

The problem of the parents here is to induce a sense of realism. It is true that life is difficult, but not nearly as hard as it appears to the Piscean. The Pisces child must learn "That life is real, life is earnest, and the grave is not its goal." Even to them as children, the other world, where they believe all is perfection, is preferable to this world, where progress is usually the result of intelligent effort.

The wise parent will instill self-confidence, outline the chances for success or failure in any piece of work undertaken, and most important, see that it is done. The direction of effort, and the completion of every piece of work started regardless of limitations, is the only system upon which to build character in the fragile, sensitive Pisces child.

*   *   *   *

This completes the outline of characteristics in the twelve Zodiacal types of children. At this point many parents will say, "That is all very interesting, and we will indeed look for the tendencies outlined, but we have always been told that our children take after us, the parents, and our parents, and all of our numerous ancestors. We have been taught about inherited tendencies. What about that? Why, my oldest son is the picture of my father!"

The answer to these assertions is that the inherited pattern is just as true as the astrological pattern. If three sons in a family all resemble the father, (most children are a physical blend—as to feature—of both parents), and are born in the sign of Scorpio, Aquarius, and Aries respectively, the features will have the physical outline of the parent. There will be a family resemblance between all three boys—but each sign-character in which they were born will blend in with the general appearance, marking it just as plainly and just as distinctively as the features of the father. The sign characters of the planets can bend themselves to blend with any inherited pattern and animate it in a different way. Therefore the mother's, father's or grandparents' characteristics notable in the child will develop along the lines of the special planetary influences by whom he or she is controled.

BUSINESS

To-day almost every able-bodied man or woman is in business or intimately connected with business people.

Since the planets in their signs and houses are such strong factors in shaping the lives of individuals, it can easily be realized that conditions—favorable, unsettled, or explosive, and especially designed to affect business—are in constant progress.

Certain signs and planets have a greater effect on the course of commerce than others, and certain types of aspects have a stimulating or a retarding influence.

The following is an outline of the forces at work among

the houses, signs and planets, all of which affect the business program on this plane.

The first house influences new enterprise.

The second house is the house of wealth, property, investments, and land.

The third house controls mind; commercial, inventive, experimental.

The fourth house environs the small business, often individually owned; also trade, export and import.

The fifth house governs theatrical enterprise and the amusement business.

The sixth house shelters the working classes, trade unions, guilds, and organized labor.

The seventh house is the house of partnership.

The eighth house is the house of wills, legacies and inheritances.

The ninth house deals with expansion, world enterprise, and legal affairs on a large scale—also speculation.

The tenth house is the house of superiors, business or professional success, and credit.

The eleventh house harbors humanitarian enterprise.

The twelfth house governs institutions, hospitals and reform.

*   *   *

When a sign tenants these houses, the influence of the house is colored by the direction of the sign energy. When a planet moves into the sign, the planet adds its character to sign and house influence. When another planet, posited in a different sign and house, makes an aspect to the first-mentioned figure, there is activity in the departments affected, and this magnetism is reflected by marked stimulation on this plane.

The signs offer special energy toward the following enterprise:

Aries energizes the pioneer in any project.

Taurus activates wealth, property holding, and real estate.

Gemini favors scientific invention, the stock market and travel by plane.

Cancer stimulates trade and transportation by water.

Leo activates the amusement business.

Virgo controls servants; also public service and health programs.

Libra governs jurisprudence and diplomacy.

Scorpio activates research, mining, engineering, etc.

`Sagittarius stimulates gambling on a large scale, world enterprise, international law, and the publishing and advertising businesses.

Capricorn controls authority and measures worldly success.

Aquarius stimulates revolutionary business methods and social programs, airplane travel and development.

Pisces governs the motion-picture industry, water travel, and the trade in drugs, chemicals and medicines.

Of the ten planets some have a very serious effect on business progress.

BUSINESS PARTNERS

Every sign of the Zodiac has some possibilities for business partnership. Some of the sign qualities make for better business partners than others. Here is a list of the signs with the characteristics to be expected in partners of that sign:

ARIES

March 21 to April 19

The Aries man is not designed for successful partnership. Rather, as has been pointed out before, he is a leader. If he should enter into a partnership, he had best be the active, resourceful, inventive member of the firm. He will be fearless, bold, too willing to take a chance, and rather rash and daring unless there is some tactfully restraining hand. It will be hard to restrain him, for he often acts without consulting anyone. He is so impatient that he cannot wait for counsel. Sometimes his judgment is good and the rapid action following a decision results in a successful coup. But just as frequently he guesses wrong, and then the damage is serious.

There is a good deal of dash and inspiration to a partnership with a high Aries type, but there is also a great element of chance. The weak Aries type is a bad bet all around. He has not the "zip" of his more noble brother, and he has a great deal of uncertainty and indecision. Then when he does act, the resulting chances rest with the gods.

TAURUS

April 20 to May 20

The Taurus person, makes in many ways an admirable partner. He may not be the "brains" of the concern, but he is the "works." The aggressive Taurus type is an admirable worker, tireless and dependable, risking everything he has to give in strength and resources. He is somewhat more conservative about the resources than he is about the effort.

His worst fault as a business partner is stubbornness. He is not brilliant, and he is not always willing to learn. He is not even willing to listen, and has, when he finally gives his attention, a very slow grasp of an idea.

However, this does not mean that the Taurus partner is a wooden, obstinate person, blind to his own benefits. Sometimes this is the case, but for the most part the Taurus type is too good a business man not to finally visualize benefits.

Therefore this steadfast, honest type when dealt with tactfully can make a satisfactory partner.

GEMINI

May 21 to June 21

Gemini natives are not built for partnership. They are so changeable and erratic that it is hard to get a decision out of them that is not subject to change, revison and dissection.

They are fussy and irritable one moment and highly animated the next. This hardly makes for a harmonious or progressive partnership.

While Gemini persons are intellectual, they are better equipped to work upon their undoubted talents alone. However, if these people should happen to form a partnership they might be considered the "head" of the concern. Usually their judgment is quick (they are very discerning) keen, and analytical. They are creative, often full of brilliant ideas that can be made extremely profitable in the hands of a practical person. For the Gemini man himself, a partnership is beneficial. Despite his many undoubted gifts, the stability necessary to conduct business, and the method is lacking in his make-up. In firms of advertising experts, publicity companies, travel bureaus, commercial artists and designers, a Gemini member to the partnership is exceedingly valuable. The creative mind, personal activity, and mental freedom from outside attachments makes them ideal for these types of business.

CANCER

June 22 to July 22

The Cancer person, unless of the aggressive type, is not good as an active partner in a business. He might possibly make a silent partner.

The aggressive type has some virtues as a partner, and as many faults. On the negative side of the ledger, they are indecisive people, moody, irritable and exacting. They cling to old methods, and are unprogressive. They change their moods, but they are unwilling to change their methods.

On the positive side of the ledger, they have a natural comprehension of business, and a good deal of business acumen. They are persistent. They have a nice understanding of finances, and really enjoy business routine. They are cooperative in daily occurrences, sympathetic, and have a sense of the dramatic.

On the whole, the aggressive Cancer type, if balanced by some one with initiative, makes a satisfactory business partner.

LEO

July 23 to August 23

The Leo person makes a good partner, if he teams up with someone who will allow him sufficient control. He is never willing to take a back seat, and if he is of the high type of Leo, he is trustworthy and capable. In a partnership, he should be the contact man. His personality is usually impressive, and he commands respect. He is dominant and forceful and can always take care of the outside interests of a concern. He has the power to win trust, partly because he is usually very sincere in whatever he attempts. He is a born showman, and can dramatize any business in a very convincing manner.

Personally he is not so easy to get along with. These natives have a wonderfully generous nature, for they will give till it hurts, not only themselves, but everybody else. They obligate people to the point of embarrassment, and do more than their share of everything. Great dissatisfaction is often the result of this unequal division of labor. Their tempers are furious, and they are far too dictatorial.

With the Leo native, the benefits far outclass the faults, provided the type is high and noble.

VIRGO

August 24 to September 23

The Virgo person is a good partner. He is painstaking, meticulous, intelligent and progressive. He is not progressive in a great sense, but in small ways he is ever willing to try the new and novel. He is modest, unassuming and co-operative. He is faithful himself, and exacts a full measure of service from his employees.

The Virgo partner will never force his will, or make his ideas prevail, but his intelligence in practical matters can be trusted.

He is fussy and fretful to a fault, and demands that every "i" be dotted, and every "t" crossed.

He complains eternally and is never satisfied, for his notions of perfection are based upon the ideal, and anything short is a disappointment to him.

LIBRA

September 24 to October 23

The Libra person is the ideal partner. Libra is the sign of partnership, and these natives are the most composed, balanced, temperate and rational of all the twelve signs.

They can adapt themselves to any personality and bring out the best in the other fellow. They never fall down on their own share of the work, and can be trusted implicitly to give an honest account of themselves. They accept the most advanced standards in whatever the field of endeavor, but they are seldom willing to adopt the extreme or the revolutionary. This is not because they are reactionary, but because they can not with perfect justice permit anyone to risk their means on an untried or unproved method or system. Intellectually they might be interested in the extreme renovation, but materially they would not be willing to take the risk.

The weak Libra type lacks direction, and passes out a good deal of smooth diplomatic talk to serve for facts and action. They are not such a good bet as a partner, and the benefits of partnership with a weak Libra person are just as doubtful as a relationship with other less productive types.

SCORPIO

October 24 to November 22

The Scorpio temperament is entirely unfit for partnership unless the character is modified by other aspects in the birth figure. They are unreasonable, tyrannical, dogmatic, and so irascible that no worthwhile partner would care to endure so much for the doubtful possibility of business success under such circumstances.

In any position but one of supreme authority, the Scorpio person discloses qualities that hardly any active type could bear for constant and progressive association.

A modified Scorpio personality is very intelligent, thorough, dependable and shrewd. It has a fine grasp of any problem, can analyze a situation, and tell in advance the extent of the possibilities for success or failure. This in itself is a wonderful quality for partnership, but the Scorpio disposition offers so many other faults for double harness that their undoubted ability does not balance. Their passions are too intense, uncontrolled and furious for the exacting demands of everyday business.

SAGITTARIUS

November 23 to December 22

The Sagittarian makes a good business partner. Natives are impersonal (in many ways) in their judgments, with the balanced quality of thought found in the Libra natives. They harmonize with the partner, and add color, drama and style to the business, whatever it happens to be. They are exceedingly energetic, and give a great deal of themselves toward making business a success.

This type of person is somewhat of a plunger, and needs a restraining hand when it comes to the new, untried and highly speculative. Very often they are out-and-out gamblers, and their keen intuitive minds generally lead them to the winning proposition.

Sagittarians are optimistic to a fault, and see only the most glowing side of a situation. The very highly developed Sagittarian is temperamentally equipped to handle great business enterprise. These people have the vision and practical imagination for vast schemes of world-wide dimensions.

CAPRICORN

December 22 to January 19

The Capricorn person is fairly well adapted to partnership. Natives are honest, dependable and tremendous workers. Their special talent is business and the whole commercial scheme. It appears from these statements that they would make exceptionally good partners, and as far as the business procedure and routine go, they are well-nigh perfect.

But the disposition of the Capricorn person is against him. The moon in Capricorn has been called the "Figure of the Devil", and though the solar position is a little less intense, the qualities are almost as forbidding.

It is hardly inviting to have a partner (however hard a worker) who is forbidding, austere (almost inhumanly so), dogmatic, and whose final word is law. Harsh, driving and severe, the manner is always dour, suspicious and unrelenting. These qualities do not make for a reasonable business relationship, no matter how much capability is brought to bear.

The Capricornians themselves prefer to work alone, and are frequently specialists in their line (whatever it is), so detailed and exhaustive are their research and study.

AQUARIUS

January 20 to February 18

Aquarians make good partners. Many of the temperamental blessings found in the Libra and Sagittarian make up are also to be met with in Aquarians. They are progressive partners, for they seem to have a special insight that guides them in scenting new trends. They themselves are very experimental, often adding some new system, or inventing an improvement that has far-reaching business consequences.

These people dislike dissension, and always avoid acrimonious argument. They are scrupulously honest, and handle money, especially other people's money, with the greatest care.

The weaker Aquarian types do not always keep their word. They exaggerate, and make impossible promises that they have no notion of keeping unless some lucky accident helps them out.

Vital Aquarians put their best efforts into a business that is not strictly commercial, but has some quality of service, or advancement for the world at large in the program.

PISCES

February 19 to March 20

The Piscean is the ideal silent partner. When actively engaged in a partnership, he is apt to be too indecisive, and either too suspicious or too trusting. His emotions invade everything and they are not clear-sighted. The Neptunian pall of delusion hangs over his reactions, and all of his judgments are apt to be clouded.

These are talented people, and their work in the several lines into which they fit has grace and charm. But they are too often unwilling to conform to accepted standards, always questioning, and weighing values in terms of the unknown.

This spiritual responsiveness can be very beautiful, but even in the most artistic business, where the values are among the arts, the commercial system prevails. Unless the Pisces nature is strengthened by other planetary combinations, they will make rather weak partners in a business venture.

It must be remembered that these summaries are general, based on solar and lunar characteristics, which in the individual horoscopes are often altered by other planetary forces. Many people follow the general characteristics of their sign, and will in most ways conform to the sign-character. Where the differences are very great, the individual birth chart must be erected.

THE ASCENDANT

The Ascendant in a horoscope is the sign rising over the horizon at the exact moment of the native's birth. The Sun of the native is placed at mid-heaven, and the sign coming up over the parallel line of the horizon is the Ascendant. The time of the native's birth is necessary for the finding of the ascendant, because of the possible planets posited in that sign at that moment. In fact, for any detailed horoscope the exact moment of birth is imperative.

Traditionally, in Astrology the ascendant shapes the personality and frequently the appearance. In many cases this influence blends with the sun sign to make a complete personality.

The qualities of the ascendant are the same as if the sun were in that sign at birth, and often when the native has a powerful solar influence at birth and an equally strong ascendant, the personality is what is called "loud."

If the solar influence is weak, and the moon not very well placed, the ascendant often carries the chart. If there are planets in the rising sign, the personality is colored by the quality of the planets in that particular sign. If these planets are unafflicted they will provide energy for accomplishment in whatever realm they activate.

When the planets in the rising sign are afflicted, it indicates possible success with life's ambitions in spite of overwhelming obstacles. This is true of any square or opposition, but since the ascendant deals primarily with life's ambitions, the inference is that a strong character will triumph in the end.

Those who feel that they do not resemble the characters outlined by the solar or lunar descriptions, or even the Venus characterization, had best seek out the exact hour of their birth, to find the ascendant of their birth figure. This can be done most accurately by consulting an ephemeris of the year of birth. Any reliable astrological publication has lists in their files of ephemeris for many years back. Seek out your year, and find the position of the different planets at the exact time of birth. Whatever sign was rising at that moment may supply the key to your character. Read our solar and lunar description for that particular sign, and you may discover what you are seeking about yourself.

It must also be remembered that many well-meaning people have a false conception of themselves, and even when presented with an accurate picture of their own personality and temperament, they cannot or will not recognize it. Most of us would rather be idealistic types, with exceptional qualities and impulses for good. But the astrological forces being impersonal influences of varying strength, it is largely up to us what we do with the energy Nature has provided for our development. If we are disappointed with the astrological picture of our characteristics, we have only to take the planetary forces in our own make-up, as outlined in the birth figure, (even the most general outline) and develop the positive value of each planetary influence. The result is bound to be good, for the amount of virture unused in this universe is storing a mighty reserve of energy that only practice will develop. Possibly the strength of the malifics comes from ages of repeated usage.

FRIENDSHIP

Each sign of the Zodiac has its own capacity for friendship. A great deal has been written on the ability to love, as bestowed by the great planetary powers, but all of the twelve signs, (some much more than others), give us some portion of this highly civilized gift for friendship.

From the earliest history of mankind many of our noblest impulses arise out of friendship, and some of the most powerful romances of the past were not built of romantic love, but of friendship. We have but to recall the passionate words of the Bible king, David, upon the death of his friend Jonathan to measure the depths of intellectual union:

"I am distressed for thee, my brother Jonathan: very pleasant hast thou been unto me: thy love to me was wonderful, passing the love of women. How are the mighty fallen, and the weapons of war perished." These words were a tribute to both men.

Therefore it is quite natural for people to wonder about themselves and seek out their own ability to be friends, and to draw friendship to them by their quality of thought.

Aries - March 21 to April 19

The Aries person seeks friendships enthusiastically, but naturally reserved and a little austere, these people appear to be giving more of themselves than they really are. They always reserve something of themselves for themselves. They disagree passionately, and cannot seem to bear with contrary opinions. While the upheaval is brief, it is often enough to chill any warmth that may have previously existed. They are so inflamed by enthusiasm that they often pursue friendship that is but a reflection of the aura created by their own qualities. In this way they are too often doomed to disappointment when the object of their friendship is seen in his or her own commonplace light. The Aries person may frequently be said to put the "interest" into friendship.

Taurus - April 20 to May 20

Taurus people make faithful, trustworthy friends. These warm-hearted people may be described as "faithful forever." They are rather inarticulate people, and value friendship, but do not always know how to capture the friends they crave. Determined and patient in all the impulses of life, they react the same way in matters of engaging friendships. They worship beauty, and love to center their devotion in the high places. In this way Taureans who are servants often become the trusted friends of their employers; and in other, less lowly walks of life, Taureans make lasting friendships among those high above them in station. They are not inspired friends, but they offer permanence and dependability to any relationship that they enlist.

Gemini - May 21 to June 21

The Gemini person does not incline to deep relationships. These people are rather impersonal, and their devotion to abstract intellectuality robs them of the taste for intimate human relationships. They can become very enthusiastic over a mental concept, or factors in a problem, but the spiritual urge toward high human relationships is rather weak in the Gemini make-up. They are almost always very pleasant people to know as acquaintances, and usually number scores of passing semi-friendships on their lists. But they are too humorously critical for the deeply sentimental, and even laugh at themselves when they approach any of the noble passions. Actually they look down upon their own emotions, for they are apt to class all emotion as sentimentality, and consequently a weakness.

Cancer - June 22 to July 22

The Cancer person often makes an admirable friend. The stronger, more vital Cancer type loves friendship, for they love to give and to serve. The danger in Cancer friendships lies in their ability to absorb the object of their interest. Such a friendship can become demanding and too enveloping, so that there is no equality, but rather a burden on one side and a dead weight on the other. But it has been said that Cancer people of the active type have a fine capacity for friendship, but in the light of this criticism, one wonders how?

The vigorous Cancer type is idealistic and inspiring. They draw people to them by a sensitivity that proclaims itself both willing to give and to receive. They may prove thin-skinned and easily insulted, but these people blossom delightfully in an atmosphere of sympathy and sincere helpfulness.

Leo - July 23 to August 23

Leo persons make noble friends. They draw great qualities to them, and are unstinted in their own giving.

The less exalted types offer the sort of friendship theoretically current in the underworld—that die-hard variety of loyalty famous for endurance under stress.

The high Leo type gives a completely devoted friendship, that when properly requited, becomes a very fine relationship. The danger to the Leo friend is that unless the other side of the friendship is an individual of equal stature, this person will become too dependent on the spiritual and sometimes material offerings of over generous Leo, and thus the fine balance, always a part of a successful friendship is hopelessly destroyed. Leo people, in all relationships are apt to give too much, thus despoiling the other side of their just right to be generous.

Virgo - August 24 to September 23

These people are rather too self-centered for the high types of disinterested friendship. They love too much to profit materially by everything that they do, and the intellectual intimacy necessary to friendship is instinctively repugnant to them. Their natural make-up does not invite confidences from others, nor do they offer them, being far too suspicious for trust, even when their chaste emotions dictate a moderate warmth.

Should the friendship of a Virgo person be gained, he or she will treat it with the meticulous honor accorded to all of their possessions.

Libra - September 24 to October 23

The Libra person makes an interesting friend. These people instinctively look upon everything in life as an art, and while they do not throw themselves into friendship with the passion put into love, they treat the relationship with the reserve and dignity that their natural predilection for partnerships suggests.

They become the friend who advises coolly, sees even the intimates not too frequently, and always puts his or her most gracious and amusing self forward. Friendship with a Libran usually has a touch of formality about it, no matter how willing they are to assume responsibilities or do favors for those they cherish. Like Aries people, they always hold something of themselves in reserve. But unlike Aries, they do not tire their friends with the weight of personality. The keynote of the friendship offered by the Libran is discretion.

Scorpio - October 24 to November 22

This powerful type has no capacity for a successful friendship. They are too violent, jealous, tyrannical and overbearing in all of their relationships. These qualities are the natural enemies of friendship, and with Scorpio natives friends fare just as badly as relatives, with the possible exception that the friends do not have to "take it", and they don't.

The Scorpio personality is interesting. It invites extremes of either love or hate, devotion or loathing. People usually feel something "strong" toward Scorpio natives, but the Scorpio person cannot maintain affections when the urge is toward devotion. Sooner or later a conflict arises that represents a difference of opinion, and then the Scorpio person destroys the relationship by an unreasonable exhibition, or an act of violence. Sometimes this character reveals depths of intrigue and complicated deceit that overwhelm and frighten other types by the very nature of their underhanded wickedness. Even those who love the native and would bear with him (or her) are unwilling to be drawn into Scorpio intrigue.

Sagittarius - November 23 to December 21

The Sagittarian is well equipped by nature for friendship. These people are extremely sociable and enjoy the give and take of intellectual society. (This of course refers to the high type Sagittarian.) The lower types are even more socially inclined, but they are boisterous, intemperate and generally not a good influence. Even among the higher orders of Sagittarian, are found the kind of person who can make license very attractive to their intimates, and at the same time rekindle their own love for revelry.

The noble Sagittarian is an intellectual stimulant to friends who learn to know real joys of companionship with the Sagittarian. They offer a friendship that is warm, worldly, active and progressive.

Capricorn - December 22 to January 19

Capricorn persons could make fast friends if they choose to do so. They might never make exciting friends, but if steadiness, fixity, and solidity were the only ingredients of friendship Capricorn people could give unsparingly. On the rare occasions where they bind themselves in friendship they are devoted forever.

Generally these people are too narrow, prejudiced, critical and cold to seek friendship, for they are somewhat like Virgo, suspicious of everything and everybody. They are more intense and violent than Virgo people, and take dislikes with far greater readiness than "likes." It can almost be said that they resent charm, and meet all grace with sour criticism and biting disdain. Naturally such a temperament would not invite friendship. Whether in their secret hearts they resent their own lack of ability to attract, and perforce assume a negative attitude, is another question, but whatever the answer, Capricorn people do not make very satisfactory friends.

Aquarius - January 20 to February 18

Aquarians have the ability to make the highest type of friends offered by any of the Zodiacal people. They have the gift for friendship, being neither jealous, possessive or too intense, but having a genuine interest in people and human relationships. Aquarians are reasonable, just, generous in a sensible fashion, with an instinctive knowledge of give and take, all of which are necessary to conduct a successful friendship. These people offer uplifting intellectual companionship, and usually bring out the very best in those they give the fine gift of their intimacy.

Aquarians are most discriminating, and while their interests are the least snobbish, they almost always choose their intimates with the greatest care. Some of the loftiest friendships are within the scope of Aquarian natives.

Pisces - February 19 to March 20

Pisces people love friendship, and frequently seek friends with more enthusiasm than good sense. They desire warmth and love and deep human contact so intensely that their will often urges them on to give and confide where a little investigation, or just plain clear sightedness, would save many heartaches. The Pisces person is apt to treat friendship rather too much like love.

These people give themselves quite freely, but they do not study the friend with realism. They expect impossible perfections often not within human range, or refuse to bear with ordinary human failings. They become disillusioned and despondent as soon as the friendship fails to be an affair of the gods. Pisceans suffer deeply because of their own inability to be satisfied with the range of human beings. The Neptune influence in the life of these people adds great confusion to their reactions. They are often blind to their own failings, which are legion, and see themselves as suffering martyrs, even when surrounded by every material comfort. Naturally, a friendship founded upon illusion and delusion is a doubtful joy.

It must always be remembered that the foregoing delineations cover only a part of the personal make-up. All of the other factors mentioned from time to time throughout this book help to round out weak or unfavorable aspects.

But if we examine ourselves and our friends from the point of view of the analysis given, we may recognize many of the tendencies outlined as part of the character of our friends, to say nothing of ourselves.

YOUR LIFE WORK HELPED BY THE STARS

One of the most ancient uses of astrology was the seeking of success. Kings consulted the stars for predictions of state-craft. Bankers sought out seers to read the stars for financial guidance. Generals searched the heavens for promises of victory. Naturally, warnings were as much a part of prediction as promises, but records show that a small percentage profits by the warnings.

In the distant past it was largely "the great" who availed themselves of the specialized guidance of the stars. The masses always feared the forces of nature, but rulers and leaders have been irresistibly drawn to consult the mysterious powers in the hope that guidance would be forthcoming.

Everybody can be guided by the stars; and what is more vital in the life than the work we choose? The choice of work can mean our happiness or unhappiness, fulfillment or failure, poverty or wealth. In almost every way our ability to live happily is wrapped up in our choice of a life work. Is it not then entirely reasonable that we study ourselves before haphazardly selecting an occupation?

How often does one meet the man or woman who during middle age sadly mentions some youthful talent that might have added to their prosperity and happiness had it been cultivated. Necessity plays a great part in these professional tragedies, necessity and the ignorance of guardians.

Today the attitude of parents is more progressive, and they themselves search out the most congenial and suitable professions for their children. Despite business depressions, and the scarcity of work, countless avenues for new professional activities have opened, so that the various tendancies of each sign character have plenty of scope.

Each sign has professional and artistic possibilities, although the medium and means of expression vary. The native should always look up the moon's position in the natal chart, and also the sign position of Venus, to form a better conception of their place in the world's work.

Aries - March 21 to April 19

Aries persons are, regardless of the choice of craft, leaders and pioneers. They have the ability to brave new fields of enterprise, conquer new worlds, and lead groups of workers, whether a sales force, or a group of South American excavators among the cliffs of the Andes Mountains. They have the soldier's temperament and may rise to high official positions through the Army, Government service, Civil Service, or Politics. Where the Arts or Professions or even business is concerned, the Aries nature furnishes the motor or energy. It is up to the other planetary indications to indicate the specialized field where this power can be put to work, for these people are exceedingly versatile, and can learn to do almost any fine ennobling work well.

Taurus - April 20 to May 20

Taurus people have an instinctive understanding for all branches of farming, planting and cultivating. They make fine gardners, horticulturists and florists. They succeed with breeding animals, and with poultry. They have scientific leanings along the lines of natural history and domestic science, and could work enthusiastically in the fields of bacteriology and dietetics. The dietician has great commercial possibilities today. Building is another field for which the Taurean is adapted, especially the construction of homes. Modern housing is a great industry, and the possibility of improvements in this line opens new vistas of progress. Last mentioned, but very important, is the Taurus gift for singing. Some of the great songsters of the world have the sun, moon or some other planet well aspected in Taurus.

Gemini - May 21 to June 21

The Gemini person is designed for success in the newspaper or publishing business, and this includes the advertising and publicity, or radio advertising fields.

They have a natural dexterity that inclines them toward dentistry or commercial art, and combined with this facility goes a searching analytical type of mind, which often makes a successful inventor.

A flow of ready speech is one of the Gemini gifts, and sometimes these people make clever lawyers and tutors.

The Gemini person with the mathematical mind turns to finance and stock operations.

Cancer - June 22 to July 22

Here we find the artists and authors and poets. The sensitivity of the Cancer native inclines them to all the arts, for the nature yearns for self-expression. Cancer people make very sympathetic actors and actresses, for they not only have the emotional urge to act, but they succeed in captivating an audience. For this reason they make splendid crusaders, especially as Cancer people almost always have a "cause" for which they are fighting or a social error that they hope to put right.

Cancer people have very good business minds combined with their art, and they fit in very well in the fields of commerce.

Scientifically they also have a place. They make excellent doctors, with marvelously sympathetic bedside manners. The original "bedside manner" of the successful physician must have belonged to a Cancer man—for they are the most tender people and almost suffer with the patient. The sensitive perceptions of these natives make them fine diagnosticians, good analytical chemists and excellent nurses.

Leo - July 23 to August 23

Leo people are most successful where they can employ their dominant and colorful personalities. They excel in the amusement field, either as actors, actresses, managers or dramatists. Any department in the amusement business suits their temperament to perfection.

As for the other arts, Leo people lean toward decoration and design. They excel as interior decorators and designers of clothes, fabrics and household furnishings.

Another outstanding gift of both sexes that may be uncovered among the Leo capabilities is the ability to cook superbly.

Virgo - August 24 to September 23

The Virgo group inclines toward statistical work. Accountancy, bookkeeping, stock-brokerage management, or any work directing the exact and conservative use of money or wealth of any kind.

Scientifically, Virgoans are adapted to medical practice,

especially in the field of germ study, and sterilization. They make active workers in public health movements, and good nurses.

As for the social sciences, these people incline toward research, history and governmental recording. They excel as teachers and, in the higher groups, preachers.

Libra - September 24 to October 23

The Libra people lean toward the arts. In the theatre they become beautiful dancers, or actors and actresses where grace and charm are essential. Sculptors, painters, and musicians are often found among Libra natives.

In governmental service the Libran chooses the Navy. The romance of sea life seems to appeal to their temperament.

In the business world Librans succeed as merchants, where their talent for selection, buying, display, tact and management gets full play.

In professional life, diplomacy, international law and judgeship, or work in any advisory capacity is quite within their talents, even if the road to some of these professions is long and arduous.

Scorpio - October 24 to November 22

These people are natural scientists and philosophers. They are "searchers." They are constantly studying the occult and mystic and working in the ruins of the world to find a key to the past that may enlighten the future. They make great chemists, mining experts, and engineers.

Since the desire to search is natural to them, a man-hunt is interesting to them. They make excellent detectives.

The Mars influence in Scorpio makes these natives very skillful with instruments. In the Scorpio group can be found some of the finest dentists and surgeons.

Sagittarius - November 23 to December 21

The Sagittarian makes a great professor, in which profession he is often called upon to be guide, philosopher and prophet. This role he is well able to undertake; in fact, any position of responsibility, where mature worldly judgment and wise counsel are needed is the right place for the Sagittarian. It is not so much the specific field chosen by the Sagittarian, as what he or she will do in that particular position. Well aspected, these people are big in stature, and likely to be successful whether they become publishers—dramatists, politicians, clergymen, or great financial manipulators. All of these professions are within their scope. The physical type excels as an athlete.

Capricorn - December 22 to January 19

The Capricorn person has been described astrologically as the specialist: the person who takes one small department in a business or profession and develops it to perfection. This gift for exactitude is outstanding in all of the works of the Capricornian.

They are exceedingly material people, and make a place for themselves in the business world. Commerce and business are their best fields of endeavor, and all other things being equal, they make great executives. The sign itself is one of high authority, and a strong Capricornian often reaches a very powerful position. In any walk of life where authority is militaristic, the Capricorn person is temperamentally at home.

Scientifically, these natives lean toward work with a mathematical background. Chemistry, military science, astronomy, and navigation are all possible for the Capricorn person.

Aquarius - January 20 to February 18

The Aquarian is the ideal college professor. These natives have wonderful intellectual equipment, and a real urge toward helping the seeking mind of the student. They are never hidebound, but quite the opposite, are always on the lookout for the progressive idea or the new thought, provided it is constructive thought.

The Aquarian is naturally an inventor, and no matter what his line, he can think of something new to help himself or the boss to the betterment of the business.

Aquarians are great social organizers and reformers. They succeed in the publishing business, and the advertising line, particularly in connection with radio. Any business or profession that deals in the distribution of knowledge or education is good for the Aquarian. They are naturally literary, and writing is a fertile field for them.

They have an urge for travel, (especially air travel), and could succeed in work connected with travel bureaus, or any agency connected with air, rail or even water locomotion.

Pisces - February 19 to March 20

In the arts, Pisceans favor poetry, humorous writing, or the more emotional types of fiction. They often make good musicians, or artists. In the dance they favor pantomime or eccentric dancing. The motion-picture field, (being a world of illusion), is especially good for the Pisces person. Neptune rules the world of illusion, and therefore the Piscean tendency is in the direction of all shadowy, dreamlike creations.

Travel by water, or any employment connected with water transportation is good for Pisces. Trade in liquids, medicines, beverages, liquors, perfumes, make-up and cosmetics (luxury trades) are all natural avenues for the Piscean to seek out for a life work.

For the highly evolved natives of this sign, social reform, especially work in prisons, medical research or attendance, and the ministry (or other church work) offer natural outlets for the spiritual, sympathetic Pisces nature.

*   *   *   *

If, by consulting our luna chart, the position of the moon is located, the aptitudes here described as belonging to sun signs, are even stronger when a similar position is occupied by the moon. Therefore, every one has, not only a complete set of inclinations and talents bestowed by the sun's position, but an even more intense selection of possibilities given by the moon. Any other planet posited in any of the twelve signs gives some quality that can be turned to commercial purposes in the life. The stars give us so many talents and tendencies that it is astonishing how little of it is used by mankind. The proportion of economic and spiritual failures in this world are all out of proportion with the gifts bestowed. Nature has helped us better than we realize, and we are incredibly lazy and stupid when we fail to find a productive niche for ourselves, considering the wealth of material that each of us has within ourselves to choose from and develop.

Naturally, most charts have oppositions and afflictions in them, so that success is never easy. It has been said that the most successful people were the ones with the greatest afflictions against major planets in the natal chart. It is the triumph of the human being over big natural principles, which may be against him, that makes greatness. It is up to every person to find his or her place in the sun. According to Astrology, no person in the world can truthfully say of anyone else, "Well, he (or she) is not really fitted for anything; there is nothing but clerking that I can think of." An honest survey of the astrological possibilities will show three or four fine avenues of commercial, artistic or professional progress for everyone. And, educational possibilities being what they are to-day, everybody has a chance.

SKELETON IN YOUR CLOSET

Doubtless every one of us has a secret weakness or a fault that might, if not corrected, cause us the loss of everything we value.

Usually these weaknesses are the result of adverse planetary positions or unfriendly planetary combinations. These conditions appear in the nativity, and all through the life they are re-irritated by the transits of the planets involved.

Some of the dangerous faults are murderous temper, intemperance, financial dishonesty, thievery, blackmail, and all the varieties of the capital crime of murder.

Many people may resent the implication that they have faults of so serious a nature, but it has been said that if a detective stepped up to any individual on the street and whispered ever so softly in his ear, "All is discovered," the person so addressed would collapse with fright.

Probably this is somewhat exaggerated, but it is a real fact that many of us have faults that we do not even try to correct, or that we regard with insufficient seriousness. How often have we heard some person say almost with pride, "Have I got a temper! Say, when I get mad, I could commit murder."

Most of the tragedies that arise from violent, uncontrolled anger are inspired by negative Mars action. When Mars is afflicted in the birth figure, or is adverse to the native sun during the life, the person involved is in danger. Such persons are in danger from their own rash actions.

The most brutal murders are often committed by Mars-afflicted natives. Types most likely to be dominated by Mars activity are people born in Aries, March 21 to April 19; Scorpio, October 24 to November 22; Capricorn, December 22 to January 19; and Leo, July 23 to August 23. These signs are very sensitive to the action of the planet Mars, because Mars rules Aries and Scorpio, is powerful in Leo and exalted in Capricorn. Therefore people with either the sun or moon in any one of the signs mentioned would be stimulated by the aspects from this planet, and particularly sensitive to mental suggestion and physical action of a Martian character. The moon gives an especially sensitive planetary influence, and those who have this Martian trend in their lives through the position of the moon are especially subject to unreasonable outbursts of uncontrolled temper and violence.

The type of excess impelled by Mars operating in each of the signs mentioned is different.

Aries People are apt to commit crimes of accident—or the type of crime that is the result of violent attack caused by anger and unwillingness to be restrained that can result only in death. The old-fashioned duellist, who dashed about waving sword or pistols at the slightest provocation, eternally wishing to defend all varieties of honor, is one of the best examples of this type.

Scorpio people commit more crimes of passion than any others. (Especially the luna Scorpions). In notorious sex crimes the principal actor of the drama usually has the moon in Scorpio (if not the sun) or some planet posited therein, unfriendly to the sun or moon. In any case, Scorpio people tend toward the sex crimes, and the *crime passionel* of continental romance has been usually enacted by a Scorpio personality. These people are deep, subtle, conniving and underhanded, as well as violent. It is impossible to fathom their motives easily, and it takes real detective skill to get at the bottom of their intricately devised crimes. The Scorpio person is the best detective as well as the cleverest criminal.

The Capricorn person is dominated by a Saturn-Mars combination. (Mars is exalted in Capricorn). These people make "hard boiled" determined, relentless criminals, who fight for bad as most people fight for good. Sometimes this planetary combination gives the native a misguided savior complex, and then they wish to destroy all "sinners" or people who love enjoyment and riotous living. Sometimes a series of "avenger murders" or "punishment murders" are carried out by this planetary type. Should the Capricorn person turn criminal, especially the Luna Capricornian, he becomes the toughest, most vicious criminal imaginable. Luna Capricorn has been called, in Astrology, "The Figure of the Devil." This suggests a temperament that can plot with complete coldness, and execute premeditated crimes that are carried out with the care and exactitude of high enterprise.

The Leo person, whether of the Solar or Lunar type is often the victim, rather than the perpetrator of the crime. This type in astrology has been likened in character to the Sun God of ancient Greek mythology, whose fate is tragic and heroic. These people often rise to great heights in the service of an idea, and through the treachery and jealousy of others are the victims of frame-ups. On such occasions, the Leo person may meet a tragic end.

The destructive influence of Mars, so powerful in the lives of the several types mentioned, is, as has been described, of a different nature with each of the signs mentioned. The Mars force is wholly physical, but, when combined with the sign-character of the several types mentioned, a different mentality is added. This individuality furnishes the key to the kind of crime each person is most likely to commit.

It must always be remembered that none of the types mentioned may ever commit crimes, but since the earthly plane does harbor criminal personalities, those astrologically most liable to commit them are here described. Another point to be remembered is that the position of the moon is more important in this diagnosis than the sun, particularly where the type of crime has an emotional foundation.

Financial dishonesty is usually the result of an afflicted Mercury or perhaps Jupiter in Gemini badly aspected. Any planet opposed when posited in Gemini may create dishonesty. Mercury in the ancient lore, was the planet of thieves, and any irregularity of this planet and its sign of Gemini will cause the native to lean toward trickery. Combinations of Mercury with the malifics, Mars and Saturn, tend in the direction of forgery, poisoned pen letters, embezzlement and blackmail.

Jupiter afflicted or combined with a Martian influence sometimes encourages thievery in the native. Negative Sagittarians make the most lying, dishonest, confidence men in the whole spectrum of crime.

In company with false Sagittarians, or the afflicted Jupiter native, is the person at the mercy of a destructive Neptune. At best, Neptune is the planet of dreams and remote aspirations solacing only the soul. On the material plane Neptunian vibrations are seldom good, and people suffering an adverse Neptune influence are the deceivers and the deceived. In fact, they are the kings of liars, cheaters and deceivers. An afflicted moon gives similar tendencies.

Some signs harboring afflicted planets incline the native toward intemperance. This means the indiscriminate use of alcoholic drinks, drugs and foods. The signs of the Zodiac that incline toward alcoholism through either the moon or the sun influence are the water signs, Pisces, Cancer, and

Scorpio. These same signs induce the indiscriminate use of drugs, especially opiates.

Leo people lean toward over-indulgence in eating, drinking, and the use of drugs.

Virgo people are animated drug stores. They believe themselves sick with every ailment under the sun, and try all the available drugs on themselves. Sometimes, when badly aspected, they try these drugs on others, and several of the world's most notorious cases of poisoning were engineered by perverted Virgo thought.

In fact, the strength of the malifics (Mars and Saturn) are such that every sign of the Zodiac suffers from a planetary weakness of some sort. The powers of Uranus and Neptune are not always used to the best interests of mankind largely because these planets are not yet entirely understood or appreciated by life on this plane.

Few of the planetary forces are good or moral in the sense that we understand morality. These forces activate, energize, and stimulate, or subdue, soothe and palliate. These urges work in different departments, sometimes in terms of right as understood by this world. But we ourselves must know and understand something of what we are up against in order to save ourselves.

We must remember that:

In Aries, it is the crime of accidental violence;

In Taurus, perhaps the furious response to determined goading (also outbursts of profanity and vile language);

In Gemini, theft, forgery, lying and financial manipulation;

In Cancer, possible overindulgence in drugs or drink, and looseness in sexual practices;

In Leo, victimization and overindulgence in food, drink, drugs and bullying intimidation;

In Virgo, miserliness, hypochondriasm, drugs and in some cases even the tendency to poison;

In Libra, homosexuality;

In Scorpio, the crimes of passion, sexual perversion, over-indulgence in drink, and drugs;

In Sagittarius, lying, fraud, embezzlement, and theft on a large scale;

In Capricorn, organized crime, crimes of violence, homicid-al maniacs;

In Aquarius, deceit through misrepresentation;

In Pisces, deception, lying, fraud, self pity, psychic degenera-tion, overindulgence in drink, drugs and sensationalism.

SIGNS THAT ATTRACT MONEY

Some astrological types attract money. Each sign has its own capacity for creating wealth, and offers the native the natural way for his or her type to attain wealth. The use of the word "wealth" does not necessarily mean abundance, because many people never become able to acquire a great deal of real property. The use of the word "wealth" right here does mean the ability to make a living. But some of the astrological signs can be translated into material action that is very profitable, and all this with less effort than is required by the remaining Zodiacal signs. However, it cannot be stressed too strongly that *each* sign has its financial potentialities, save that some of them are more readily and naturally productive of money.

Since the earning capacity is part of the native's life ambition, the Sun sign is a better guide to fortune than the Moon's sign in the nativity. The sign of the moon is productive of sudden flurries of plenty, but the swinging of the great wheel of fortune rests with the power of the life-giver, the hot golden Sun.

The following signs seem, in very different ways to attract money:

Taurus is the sign of wealth, and carries with it considerable luck on the score of money for its natives. Most Taureans enjoy the struggle for existence, and work for the love of labor. In addition to this natural tendency to productivity, the natives of Taurus often inherit money, or enjoy benefits and gifts of large sums during the life-time donated by generous friends and relatives. In fact, these people seem to get financial help whenever they need it. Taureans, or those with important planets posited in Taurus usually amass a great deal of money and property in the course of a lifetime. Natives of Taurus born in humble circles where great opportunities never reach them always manage to get security and respectibility for themselves and their families.

The sign of Cancer gives its natives of the more forceful type a natural business intelligence. They seem to have a highly developed perception of how to do business, and both sexes, no matter how visionary and impractical they appear to be, are well able to make their commercial lives profitable. They are not people who welcome new opportunities, in fact they abhor change, but in the general routine of accepted business life they are clever, acute, perceptive and well able to grasp opportunities and manipulate money.

The sign of Virgo is exceedingly acquisitive, and attracts money steadily in a small way for its natives. Virgo people have this acquisitive sense highly developed in their personality and can pile up a fortune with pennies, day by day. It may be a miser's fortune, but by every trick of multiplication the fortune accumulates. In addition, the temper of Virgo is harmonious to business, and its natives adapt themselves readily to the commercial scheme. As a matter of fact, they revel in business. They are such cold impersonal people that they grasp with enthusiasm an intimacy that can be cherished

without embarrassing personal immolations. Business is their one passion.

The sign of Scorpio very often gives money through inheritance. These fortunes are sometimes dissipated before they ever reach the benific, but since the sign-character is preserving by nature, and the Scorpio influence protective where money is concerned, the inheritance has a fair chance of reaching the native before life is over.

The sign of Sagittarius, particularly when housing its own planet Jupiter, unafflicted, is a splendid augury for fortune. Sagittarius gives the most expansive money vibrations of the Zodiac, and multi-millionaires and international bankers almost always have, if not the Sun, one of the important planets well aspected in Sagittarius. For those Sagittarians who do not become very wealthy, there is usually great comfort derived from a productive profession,—in any case a certain degree of plenty and luxury is a certainty in the Sagittarian life.

The sign of Capricorn is the sign of success,—and also the sign of business. In that case it is easy to understand why its natives, whether they have the Sun or the Moon in Capricorn, are usually successful in the material things of life. Capricorn men, and even Capricorn women, know how to make money. They may not be brilliant or creative or unusual in any way, but they can discipline themselves and endure privations in order to accomplish a purpose or an ambition. With Capricorn people, this ambition is often material, and therefore, when the outcome is increased income it is entirely in keeping with the sign character. By steadiness, perseverance, faithfulness and detailed application, Capricornians can attain wealth where the most gifted and brilliant types just miss the mark, or fail entirely.

These signs of the Zodiac are the positions that with reasonable effort attract money. The other signs of the Zodiac have great possibilities but they depend on different qualities in the native's make-up to bring financial success. For instance, Aries is the sign of beginnings and it can be easily understood that with a beginning there is seldom wealth. Therefore the Aries person has to use his energy and power, (for these people have a power complex) and qualities of leadership to build a project, or whatever they hope to do with life, for financial success. Their force of character must be harnessed to something productive, a business or profession, which some other sign in the horoscope will indicate, in order to attain wealth.

The sign of Gemini denotes mind. It is quite true that mind is behind all expression, but the impersonal quality of the Gemini mind must also be the motor behind the Gemini native's success. Gemini people are talented, versatile, and show several aptitudes, so that even if the sign itself is not a money sign, the qualities of thought indicate growth and development. Surely this can be interpreted in physical life in terms of wealth.

The Leo person is by nature an idealist. It is a well-known fact that money is not often the outcome of pure idealism. If Leo persons would be rich, they frequently must modify or totally destroy their secret heart. If they are lucky enough to get into a business or profession that they like, the struggle is lessened. The amusement business has always been the natural field for Leo. They seem to sacrifice less and satisfy more of their deeper cravings when they serve the public and contribute to the enjoyment of the world. This service to humanity has not the intellectual quality of Aquarius, or even the sympathetic urge of Pisces. Leo's service to the public is wholly emotional, and is connected with entertainment, sports, and good times in general. Actors, actresses, theatrical impressarios, (and that covers all managers, producers and directors,) frequently have the Sun or the Moon or some other important planet in the sign of Leo.

The Libra person is in somewhat the same position as the Leo person. Librans are very artistic people, and have a natural impulse to create or to express beauty through some artistic medium. Since Libra is the sign of partnership, the Libra person usually does his work with a desire to share his expression, or go into partnership with the whole race of mankind. If he is an architect, the world uses his productions. If he is a dancer, and Libra people are often professional dancers, he usually has a dancing partner. Therefore, in any field that the Libran devotes himself to, he does it best in partnership. Like the Gemini person, Librans are intellectual and talented, and while the hard material money sense may be lacking, their creations and gifts are such that sooner or later in the life of the Libran, money is the natural result.

Aquarians do not care for money. Their capabilities are of a very high order and frequently result in plenty of money, but the chase for the accumulation of the dollar itself is not in the Aquarian make-up. The sign of Aquarius is the highest mental octave in the Zodiac, and as such makes the development of thought in the world of today the most important thing in the Aquarian's life. Since the natives of this sign are usually engaged in intellectual professions, or in businesses dealing with advancement and education, it can readily be seen that money for itself alone is a secondary consideration. Of course it must be remembered that advancement and progress have their own high price in the world, and therefore a progressive, original mind can usually be trusted to make money.

The Pisces person attracts money by suggestion. This is not entirely an attempt to be humorous, for Pisces people are the most psychic in the Zodiac. On a more mundane plane, Pisces people may be described as the most insinuating of the types. They can subtly convey their desires and ask for what they want without words, and their desires are plentiful. They are luxury loving and indulgent to themselves in the extreme, and seldom rely on their own talents, which are usually manifold, for support. There is usually a bit of the parasite in the Pisces nature, and Pisceans can make those who are devoted to them, in popular language, "come across." On the other hand, there is a very different type produced by Pisces, and this kind of person might be described by the old-fashioned word of martyr. The self-sacrificing Piscean strips himself of everything and devotes body and soul to mankind. Neither money nor material conditions count for anything. Such persons live for service, and in the solemn history books there are numberless personalities who are Piscean martyrs and have given their lives in the service of an ideal.

SIGNS THAT ATTRACT LOVE

Every one of the twelve signs has its own capacity for love, but some of the signs are especially sympathetic and suggest early marriage or happy marriage. Naturally, as in all other parts of the character and experience, the one figure mentioned here is but a part of the whole nativity, which must be interpreted as a unit to give a complete picture of the native's make-up and destiny.

The signs of Libra, Taurus, Pisces, Cancer and Leo invite and attract love, so that people with the Sun, Moon or Venus posited in any one of these signs find romantic love to be very important in the life, and exceedingly responsive to their particular type.

When the sun is posited in any of the signs mentioned, it indicates your ambitions and hopes regarding love.

When the Moon is posited in any of the signs mentioned, it indicates your attitude and point of view toward love.

When Venus is posited in any of the signs mentioned, it shows what and how you love; in other words, your manner of expressing love.

The Sun in the sign of Taurus (ruled by Venus) suggests the ambition and the power to attract a rich, handsome marriage partner. To attain a setting of luxury for love is one of the urges of this figure.

The Moon in Taurus indicates a conventional masculine attitude toward love. If this figure is found in the chart of a woman, it implies that she accepts and is guided by traditional standards regarding love. She plays the game according to the social code. This code, according to the Moon in Taurus, is confirmation of the prevailing standards of courtship and marriage, but private acceptance of sexual irregularities outside of marriage.

Venus in Taurus indicates a deep appreciation of, and response to wholesome beauty; also the desire and power to respond to the demands of love with constant virility.

The sign of Libra (ruled by Venus) is very sensitive to love, but the vibrations of Libra are more involved than the simple direct responses of Taurus.

When the Sun is found in Libra, your romantic ambitions seek love or marriage as an ideal partnership.

When the Moon is posited in Libra, your attitude toward love balances the responsibility for satisfactory love and marriage between the sexes. Your beliefs are apt to follow the old epigram of Oscar Wilde, "Manners before morals." You are more particular about a lover's behavior than his intentions.

Venus in Libra calls forth the most exquisite expressions of love.

You will be apt to express your love with the greatest delicacy, but you may also resort to extremes in physical union.

Variety of expression seems to be a talent with you, and you put everything you can bring of grace, invention and beauty into the love play.

This figure in the birth chart can be dangerous, and as has been implied under other topics, the degenerate Libran leans toward homosexuality or prostitution.

Venus is exalted in the sign of Pisces, and therefore natives of this sign are extraordinarily responsive, and attractive to vibrations of love.

The Sun in Pisces directs the ambitions toward love of a deeply spiritual nature.

You fervently believe that you seek a love that will be a completely spiritual union. Naturally, the physical is important to you too, but you expect to arrive at your best physical expression through a complete union of the spirit.

The Moon in Pisces gives you an attitude of veneration toward your love. You trust in the love that has captured your belief, and if it should fail you, the psychic consequences to yourself will be very sad.

The venerable philosophers tell us that no one ever died of love, but when people with the Moon or even Venus in Pisces suffer a love betrayal, they have been known to die spiritually. Regeneration in these cases is rare. The original trusting, believing state of mind is seldom recaptured.

Venus in Pisces expresses love with delicate ecstasy.

Your behavior may be more personal and emotional than that of a Libran, but it resembles this expression in esthetic response. In any case, you will be infinitely more loving and sentimental, and treat the beloved with more consideration and sympathy than any other type. You have the urge to serve the beloved, rather than to be served.

The Sun in Cancer directs the romantic ambitions toward seeking a mate who will help to build a home and share the responsibilities of parenthood.

The Moon in Cancer develops your protective instincts, and makes you express your thought in a protective attitude toward the beloved.

Venus in Cancer indicates a rather sensual expression of love.

Despite your urge toward family life, you are sensual rather than passionate, and your physical expressions are not as high as your mental aspirations. You might with this figure find yourself the servant of your senses, but you will also have considerable poetry, sympathy and sentiment toward the beloved.

The sign of Leo is not a part of the Venus personality. But the rulership of the Sun in this sign makes Leo passionate and dominant in the love life. The Leo ambition in this department of the life is to capture (note the use of the word "capture") an inspiring, romantic love, and the whole performance to be a breathless adventure.

The Moon in Leo dictates an attitude of great chivalry towards the beloved.

You will regard the loved one with considerable tenderness, and behave, outwardly at any rate, like a knight from King Arthur's court.

This figure is perhaps one of the only love positions in the Zodiac that does not lend itself to perversions of any kind. While the native may be adventurous and seek variety, the love behavior will be above reproach.

Venus in Leo compels extravagantly passionate expression.

You will throw yourself wholeheartedly into your love life, and give every ounce of strength, devotion, passion and loyalty to the love of that particular moment.

This does not mean that you are constantly changing your love, but it does suggest that the life can hold more than one intense love affair, which may be treated by you with increasing seriousness as the years advance.

Your general response to love may be considered the most passionate in the Zodiac. There is something sacrificial in your attitude toward the beloved, and you almost seem to court betrayal. You throw yourself into a love affair with most magnificent passion, and give the whole adventure a rapturous "all for love" flavor. You recover miraculously from the keenest romantic disappointments.

It is hardly possible to complete a passage on the special planetary responses to love without a word about the sign of Scorpio.

The sex urge is stronger in Scorpio than any other sign in the Zodiac, and consequently these people attract sexual experience.

Luna Scorpions may feel that their impulses are just as loving as those of Pisces or Libra, but this is not so. At best their impulses are all for the preservation of the race; at the worst, sexual overindulgence, and extremes in sexual practices.

The remaining signs of the Zodiac, namely, Aries, Gemini, Virgo, Sagittarius, Capricorn, and Aquarius, radiate a different sort of love interest.

With Aries, it is the love of conquest. With Gemini, and Virgo it can hardly be called love at all, especially in the sense that we understand strong romantic love. In Sagittarius it is the love of humanity. In Aquarius it is the love of the life principle, and in Capricorn it is the love of self.

REASONS FOR MOODS

> "In sooth, I know not why I am so sad:
> It wearies me; you say it wearies you;
> But how I caught it, found it, or came by it,
> What stuff 'tis made of, whereof it is born,
> I am to learn;
> And such a want-wit sadness makes of me
> That I have much ado to know myself."

With these prophetic words Shakespeare opened *The Merchant of Venice*. Not only do they foreshadow the trend of the play and suggest the theory that coming events cast their shadows before them, but they describe the mental state of us all at frequent intervals.

How to explain it and how to fight it? That is the question. Many of us know when we are suffering from a passing mood, but are none the less depressed. Others, unaware that they are victims of emotional manipulation, try to live a routine life or perhaps settle important matters when their normal judgment is not functioning.

Certain astrological types are receptive subjects for moods, fears and worries. Naturally there are degrees of susceptibility, and the birthchart determines which of the sun signs make the native succumb more readily to aspects of fear and worry as life advances.

It is very hard to unbalance a person born in the sign of Aquarius, Leo, Taurus or Scorpio. Their natural make-up gives them qualities that withstand hysteria. In the case of Aquarius it is superior mental equipment coupled with selflessness that disarms fright. With Leo, it is a kingly sense of power and safety, and the moral conviction of inward. strength. With Taurus it is a solid effort of will and earthy strength against unseen foes. With Scorpio it is an uncanny occult understanding of the unknown. Scorpio natives can meet the forces of darkness and the mysterious lords of unworthy impulse on their own ground. It is the most occult of the signs, and has an innate understanding of moods and impulses.

The signs of Aries, Libra and Capricorn come next in the strength to throw off worry and fear.

But the signs of Gemini, Virgo, Sagittarius, Cancer and Pisces are the weakest and most susceptible to aspects of threatened disaster.

There are several reasons for this, and we shall try to explain them. These are what is known as mutable signs, meaning inconstant and capable of or susceptible to change. The one exception in this group is Cancer. Cancer is not a mutable sign, but it is ruled by the moon, whose influence gives a variable, changeable, timid nature, all of which certainly leans toward fear and worry.

Therefore we may say that people with birthdays in

Aquarius, Leo, Taurus and Scorpio can control worry during the life. The people born in the signs of Aries, Libra and Capricorn find the strength to fight moods and fears. But the people with birthdays in Gemini, Virgo, Sagittarius, Cancer and Pisces succumb to the demons of the blues.

To know this is a large part of winning the battle. People with birthdays in susceptible signs will realize that these troubles which appear to be overpowering are like shadows, greatly magnified and often entirely unreal.

The planets whose influence creates worry, depression, fears, in total, "the blues," are Saturn, Neptune, Mars and the Moon. On the other hand, Venus and Jupiter (especially Jupiter) are the "pepper-uppers" of the Zodiac.

If any of these four depressing planets are afflicted in the nativity, the person is a natural-born worrier. But even if this is not the case, during the life all of the aforementioned do make unfavorable aspects to the natives' sun and other natal positions and progressed positions. This means that for a few hours, if it is the moon, to almost six weeks at a stretch, if it is Saturn, the native will be subject to lessened vitality, pessimistic thought, hysteria, and melancholia.

The native has two courses open. He (or she) may force the unwilling spirit and body into action, and knowing the mood is a false one try to face life with an imitation of the usual responses.

The second course is to rest. No action—no decisions—no pretenses. Behave as if living through a dream, and upon awakening take up the thread of action.

This may be difficult, but a course of conduct is always possible in a thoughtful life.

Saturn is the greatest single influence in the Zodiac to create false fears, exaggerated terrors, and pervade the life with an atmosphere of ominous expectancy. If Saturn is posited in Gemini, Virgo, Sagittarius or Pisces in the Nativity, the person will be subject to dour moods and an exaggerated concept of danger.

The cycle of Saturn is approximately twenty-eight years, the time it takes the planet to make the complete circle of the Zodiac. The critical periods of Saturn come every seven years, when it is in square aspect, opposition or transiting the sign in which one was born. When it is making the two-and-one-half year transit of one's birth-sign, the mood can be one of great depression and discouragement. Successful accomplishment seems denied or delayed, and there can be losses, separation, and physical depletion. Even if this "school-teacher" of the Zodiac brings rewards for faithful efforts in the past, the greater responsibilities often rest heavily on the spirit. Extra rest, a disciplined program, and determination not to give in to self-pity will help to maintain poise through this period.

The moon is perhaps the best known of all the makers of moods. When the moon is afflicted in the nativity the person is fanciful, apprehensive and a worrier all his life.

Since the moon passes swiftly through the signs, she may be said to act as a messenger of mood. The nature of the moon is absorbing, reflective and retentive. In this passage from sign to sign she releases as well as collects.

Some of these collected influences are dispersed in transit, and other qualities are absorbed for future release. Consequently everyone is subject to a variety of changing impulses, unreasonable and often unexplainable. This energy dispersed by the moon accounts for the mood of the moment—the strange, swift change of thought, often irrational, sometimes intuitive, but all of it founded upon the lunar tides.

This ebb and flow of activity is an important function of the moon, astrologically, as it is the ruler of human energy. Periods of rest, inactivity, quiet and inertia come during the decrease of the moon. With the full moon comes action, agitation, and a general release of violent energy. With this outward flow of life comes a climax. It may be for good or bad according to the nature of the planets coloring the lunar tide.

The moon controls all the fluids of the body and this includes the adrenal glands. When the body fluids are at low ebb, weariness, depression and melancholia result. This secession accompanies the wanning moon. With a full moon comes the return of vitality. Should the action of Venus or Jupiter govern this lunar tide a vast release of optimism, joy and constructive energy results. Jupiter, of all the planets, is the benefic and the harbinger of hope.

GLOSSARY

Consult this glossary for the meaning of words you do not understand. The astrological meaning of these words often differs somewhat from the accepted dictionary definition of the term.

AFFLICTED. Suffering a subtraction of original force or power. Limited functioning.

ASCENDANT. The astrological sign (often containing planets) that is rising over the horizon at the moment of an individual's birth.

ASPECT. An expression of energy from one planet to another.

ASTROLOGY. The science of prediction, based upon the influence of the stars upon the lives of men and women.

BENIGN. A gracious, harmonious, friendly influence (used in relation to a planetary aspect.)

BIRTH CHART. A diagram depicting the exact position in the heavens of all the planets on the date of an individual's birth.

BIRTH FIGURE. A single part of the birth chart; the position of one planet or any group of planets in this chart.

CHART. A diagram of the birth chart, or any other astrological picture dealing with the meaning or arrangement of the heavenly bodies.

CONJUNCTION. The meeting of two or more planets in the same space or sector of the Zodiac.

CUSPS. The imaginary astrological lines dividing the heavenly houses from each other. The word *cusp* is also used to divide the signs of the Zodiac from each other.

CYCLE. A sequence of events started by certain planetary aspects, and completing itself at the end of this expression of energy.

DEPARTMENT. A division or field of endeavor in the affairs of men represented by a sign of the Zodiac.

DUAL PERSONALITY. (Used in reference to heavenly sign-characters) Two distinct types, or a sharp character contrast included in the personality of one sign; as, in Gemini, the Heavenly Twins represent sunshine and tears, or honesty and duplicity in one nature.

DUAL RULERSHIP. The rulership of two planets over one sign, as (a) Neptune and Jupiter have a rulership in Pisces; (b) the rulership of one planet over two signs, as Mercury ruling Gemini and Virgo.

ENERGY. Activity. A planetary force radiating from the planets to man making the individual function actively for good or evil.

ENVIRONMENT. "A place where." Used largely in connection with the heavenly houses. A definite atmosphere emanating a specialized quality of thought.

EPHEMERIS. A dated table showing the exact hourly motion of all the planets, their latitude, longitude and phenomena.

EXPANSION. A growing, constructive, generous influence.

EXPLOSIVE. A violently disruptive quality of thought, sudden, over-energetic and destructive.

FORECAST. A prediction of coming events (usually for a limited future period). These predictions foretell human fortunes as based on astrological forces. Observation and usage have measured this planetary magnetism into a guide for foretelling the affairs of men.

HARMONIOUS. Smooth progress in the life surrounded by sympathetic conditions.

HEALING CRISIS. The turning point at the climax of a serious situation or tragedy. The moment at which regenerative planetary forces interfere during a degeneration, and rebuilding begins.

HEAVENLY HOUSE. A stationary section of thirty degrees in the heavens. There are twelve of these heavenly houses, each having a definite atmosphere that exercises control in its special sphere in life and events on this plane.

HORIZON. An imaginary circular line of the celestial sphere.

HOROSCOPE. A description of the heavens, written as of the time and place of an individual's birth. The horoscope contains interpretations of all of the planets in their signs and houses in relation to the person involved in order to determine the destiny.

INFLUENCE. A force leaning in a definite direction. A strong magnetic urge of a special quality.

LUNA. The moon.

LUNAR. Pertaining to the moon.

LUNAR CHART. A delineation of character and events in an individual's history as influenced by the sign and house position of the moon in the nativity.

LUNATION. A period of about one month, from one new moon to another. A type of aspect or planetary attraction.

MAGNETIC. Having great power to attract.

MALIFIC. Naturally antagonistic and generating evil influences.

NATAL. Pertaining to the day of birth.

NATAL CHART. The horoscope.

NATIVE. The name given to a person in his own birth chart. A way of referring to people in astrological conversation.

NATIVITY. The birth chart, horoscope, or natal chart. A picture or description of the heavens at the time of an individual's birth.

NEGATIVE. An opposing quality of thought. A futile indecisive influence.

OPPOSITION. (Used astrologically in connection with aspects). A barrier. An obstacle. A separating force. An expression of strongly conflicting energy and divergent circumstances.

POSITIVE. An atmosphere of co-operation, and active harmony.

POSIT. (Used in connection with the position of a planet). To place.

PLANE. This planet—the earth.

PLANET. A heavenly body that is a part of the solar system, and revolves in an orbit around the sun.

PROGRESSION. The passage of a planet from one sign on to the next. The planet is said to progress.

QUINCUNX. An aspect formed from one planet to another that reflects on the affairs of this plane in a mildly constructive manner.

RAY. (Cosmic ray). A magnetic force emanating from the planets and directed toward earthly development.

READING. The explanation of an individual horoscope.

SEMI-SEXTILE. A mildly favorable planetary aspect.

SENSATIONALISM. Impure sexual practices. A quest for notoriety under unflattering circumstances.

SEXTILE. A gentle, harmonious, profitable planetary aspect especially noted for the bringing of opportunities.

SIGN RULER. A planet that governs a sign. Each planet is most powerful in one particular sign. The planet in its own ruling sign is at the height of its magnetism. The sign qualities are harmonious to, and inspire the planet that is the sign ruler.

SIGN. A section of space in the zodiac of signs determined by the phenomena of the vernal equinox. These signs are made of twelve equal divisions of thirty degrees of the earth's orbit around the sun. They are still named for the original constellations of the ancients, from which they have separated. Each sign is a departmental representative in the life, and indicates, how (the method) the best results can be obtained in the conduct of its own phase of the existence.

SOLAR. Pertaining to the sun.

SOLAR CHART. (Or reading). A prediction of events and a description of character in an individual's chart based upon the relationship of all the other planets to the sun's position in the chart.

SQUARE. An expression of obstacles—violent opposition, limitation, and frustation.

TENANT. The occupation or residence of a planet in an astrological sign and house.

TRANSIT. The passage of a planet through the signs.

TRINE. A progressive, "lucky" influence facilitating unexpected advancement and benefits in the life.

ZODIAC. (a) Generally a reference to the twelve heavenly constellations through which the sun travels at the rate of about one degree per day.

          (b) Astrologically, the earth's orbit around the sun.

          (c) The astrological zodiac is the zodiac of the signs which are individually exactly thirty degrees of the earth's orbit around the sun.